5-95

The Words

I carry boulders across the day
From the field to the ridge,
& my back grows tired.
A few, stubborn, in a field drawn
To old blood by the evening sun
& trembling muscles, remain.
These chafe my hands,
Pull away into the black soil.
I take a drop of sweat
onto my thumb,
Watch the wind furrow its surface,
Dream of a morning
When my furrows will shape this field,
When these rocks will form my house.
Alone, with heavy arms,
I listen thru the night to older farms.

—*Gene Fowler*

D1397610

© 1965 by Gene Fowler. Reprinted from
Field Studies (El Cerrito, Calif.:
Dustbooks, 1965) by permission of the author.

Bell & Cohn's

Handbook of Grammar, Style, and Usage

Second Edition

James K. Bell
Adrian A. Cohn
College of San Mateo

Glencoe Publishing Co., Inc.
Encino, California

Collier Macmillan Publishers
London

Copyright © 1976 by Benziger Bruce & Glencoe, Inc.

Earlier edition copyright © 1972 by Glencoe Press,
A division of Macmillan Publishing Co., Inc.

Printed in the United States of America

All rights reserved. No part of this book may be
reproduced or transmitted in any form or by any
means, electronic or mechanical, including
photocopying, recording, or by any information
storage and retrieval system, without permission in
writing from the Publisher.

Glencoe Publishing Co., Inc.
17337 Ventura Boulevard
Encino, California 91316

Collier Macmillan Canada, Ltd.

ISBN 0-02-470630-2
Library of Congress catalog card number: 75-14919
  56789   83 82 81 80

For Jonathan
and for Sara

Preface

To the Student

The first edition of *Bell & Cohn's Handbook* represented an effort to cut through the gloom and verbosity, the thick ghastly pall, of the "major" college handbooks. Too often such books, in our experience, did not clarify matters: they darkened them, leaving our own students more confused and discouraged than ever, and requiring, consequently, more work and encouragement on our part, and manifold apologies. And so our book was to be different: both plain and witty, or if not witty, at least lighthearted.

Students and teachers alike have responded favorably.

"Why didn't we have such a book before?" some asked.

Others said, "At last!"

Thus in this our little *Handbook,* in its Second Edition, we have not tried to make a thing shiny new, nor have we changed for the sake of change: we have tried to improve the book that has guided, in its imperfect way, thousands of students through perhaps millions of writing problems over the past several years. We have tried to make a direct, simple, and practical book even more useful.

We have done this in large part by trying to answer in print questions our students have asked us in class. In a very real sense, therefore, the "new" *Bell & Cohn's Handbook* has become even more a series of conversations—teacher to student, but also writer to writer—on the art of writing public prose (as distinguished from less formal kinds of writing). We have changed some entries for the sake of clarity; we have added new entries to speak directly of matters ignored or treated tacitly the first time around; we have made extensive cross-references for the student who might be truly lost, or might want more related information, or might simply be browsing. In addition we have included three new features that should allow us to retain the brevity and rigorous pragmatism of the first edition and make our *Handbook* even more useful—and still easier to use—in the new edition. Appendix A offers a perspective on the research paper, including important notes on the documentation of research materials. Appendix B presents a glossary of usage, including words often confused and misused. Finally, we have concluded with a thorough index that covers every aspect of the book.

In concept and in practice, then, *Bell & Cohn's Handbook* is a pocket companion to the art of writing. We have tried to clarify and simplify, and if, in the process of doing so, we seem to have made the book strongly prescriptive, that is only because we are too acutely aware of the horde of exceptions to each rule or convention governing "correct" prose, and in that awareness we have eliminated options and exceptions for the sake of the plain and direct answer.

Using this book is simple. Besides the appendices referred to above, there is the major portion of the book, the entries.

You can use the entries as you are writing to check on such diverse matters as grammar, punctuation, style, organization, development, and manuscript preparation. Simply look up the appropriate article as you would look up a word in your dictionary.

You can also use this book when you correct and revise your essays after your instructor has marked them. As a general rule, you will find that he has marked each mistake with one of the abbreviations or symbols listed inside the covers of the book. Begin by noting the article that the abbreviation or symbol refers to. Next find the article (arranged alphabetically, of course, like the entries in a dictionary) and read it through. As you read, try to locate those parts that apply particularly to the mistakes you have made. Study these parts carefully. Analyze the examples. Then analyze your own mistake—and correct it.

If you use this *Handbook* conscientiously, you should find one day that you can get along quite well without it. That too is part of its purpose.

James K. Bell
Adrian A. Cohn

ab

Abbreviations—Use abbreviations sparingly. Write out most words in full.

Use abbreviations for:

1. Common titles followed by proper names:

    Dr. Andrew Green

    Mr. Edward Marshall

    Mrs. Edward Marshall

    St. James

2. Academic degrees:

    Ph.D.

    M.D.

    B.A.

3. *Jr.*, *Sr.*, and *Esq.* following proper names:

    Jonathan Edwards, Jr.

    Robert E. Baker, Sr.

    Ashley Brown, Esq.

4. The names of certain agencies, organizations, and institutions (omitting periods and spaces):

HEW

FBI

USC

CIA

UNESCO

5. Selected technical terms, scientific words, and trade names:

DDT

FM

UHF

mph

rpm

OED *(Oxford English Dictionary)*

6. *Ante meridiem* and *post meridiem:*

6:15 a.m. (or 6:15 A.M.)

7:00 p.m. (or 7:00 P.M.)

7. Before Christ and *anno domini* ("in the year of the Lord"):

500 B.C.

1776 A.D

July 21, 1969 A.D.

8. Common Latin expressions:

cf. *(confer,* "compare")

e.g. *(exempli gratia,* "for example")

etc. *(et cetera,* "and others," "and so on")

i.e. *(id est,* "that is")

Do not abbreviate titles when they are used without names.

ORIGINAL

The Dr. is here.

REVISION

The doctor is here.

Dr. Green is here.

Do not use abbreviations (especially etc.) merely to save time and space.

ORIGINAL

After a long ride on the subway, we finally reached downtown Lon. & went to look for a rest., where we ate steak, etc. It wasn't long before I began to think of my Tums back in the hotel rm.

REVISION

After a long ride on the subway, we finally reached downtown London and went to look for a restaurant, where we ate steak and kidney pie, mashed potatoes, cabbage, and broiled tomatoes. It wasn't long before I began to think of my Tums back in the hotel room.

---

adj

Adjectives—Use an adjective to modify ("describe" or "limit") a noun or pronoun.

1. Noun

   Violent movies are suddenly very *popular.* (The adjectives *violent* and *popular* modify the noun *movies.*)

2. Pronoun
   They are *successful,* some psychologists say, because such movies satisfy our need to be hurt. (The adjective *successful* modifies the pronoun *they.*)

Do not use an adverb in place of an adjective to complete a linking verb.

For example, consider the following sentence: "After a few drinks, she became the life of the party; but the next morning she felt *badly* and looked *terribly*." Does the sentence *sound* right to you? Your ear for language should tell you that *"felt bad"* and *"looked terrible"* are the natural expressions, all considerations of grammar aside. But there *is* a grammatical problem here: *felt* and *looked* are linking verbs; *badly* and *terribly* are adverb forms; and these forms cannot be used to "complete" linking verbs. The reason lies in the nature and function of the linking verb.

Linking verbs join (or "link") nouns or pronouns to the words that follow the verb. The most common linking verbs are forms of the verb *to be: am, are, is, was, were, would be, have been,* etc. Other linking verbs denote appearance, condition, or sensation: *appear, become, seem, look, feel, smell, sound, taste,* etc. Usually, such verbs present no difficulty:

> The room was *elegant.* (The noun *room* is joined to the predicate adjective *elegant* by the linking verb *was.)*

> The gift seemed *perfect.* (The noun *gift* is joined to the predicate adjective *perfect* by the linking verb *seemed.)*

> The escargots smelled *good,* and they tasted *delicious.* (The noun *escargots* is joined to the predicate adjective *good* by the linking verb *smelled.* The pronoun *they* is joined to the predicate adjective *delicious* by the linking verb *tasted.)*

However, many linking verbs may also function as other types of verbs. Consider, for instance, the uses of *feel:*

1. *Feel* as a linking verb:

> I *felt* wonderful after taking three aspirins. (The linking verb *felt* joins the pronoun *I* to the predicate adjective *wonderful.*)

2. *Feel* as a transitive verb (expressing action on a direct object):

> She was the sort of old lady who carefully *felt* every peach in the bin before buying her apple. (The verb *felt* is not a linking verb. It expresses action; it is modified by the adverb *carefully;* and it takes a direct object, *peach.*)

3. *Feel* as an intransitive verb (expressing action without taking a direct object):

> Jonathan *felt* under the table with his bare feet, and some friendly toes tickled his. (The verb *felt* is not a linking verb. It expresses action, and it is modified by the adverbial phrases *under the table with his bare feet,* but it does not have a direct object.)

You must recognize a linking verb, then, by its *function:* it joins a noun or a pronoun to the words that follow. And to complete a linking verb you must not use an adverb in place of an adjective.

ORIGINAL
After a few drinks, she became the life of the party; but the next morning she felt *badly* and looked *terribly.* (The adverb forms should not be used to complete the linking verbs *felt* and *looked.*)

REVISION
After a few drinks, she became the life of the party; but the next morning she felt *bad* and looked *terrible.* (The adjective forms should be used to complete the linking verbs *felt* and *looked.*)

(See **Adverb.**)

adv

Adverbs—Use an adverb to modify ("describe" or "limit") a verb, an adjective, or another adverb.

1. Verb:

    An old woman in gold-lamé stretch pants and glittering high heels *suddenly* danced across the street, moving to a tune that only she could hear. (The adverb *suddenly* modifies the verb *danced*.)

2. Adjective:

    Ruth is a *very* lovely, *very* gentle girl. (The adverb *very* modifies the adjectives *lovely* and *gentle*.)

3. Other Adverbs:

    He speaks *rather* slowly. (The adverb *rather* modifies the adverb *slowly*.)

Do not carelessly confuse adjective and adverb forms.

As a general rule, adverbs are formed from adjectives by the addition of *-ly*. But most grammarians recognize that there is no clear-cut distinction between adjectives and adverbs. For instance, the word *well* (the adverb corresponding to the adjective *good*) may be used as either an adjective or an adverb, depending on its function and meaning: "Tom Wolfe writes *well*" (that is, "with skill"); "I am *well* now" (that is, "in good health"). In the first example, *well* is an adverb; in the second, *well* is an adjective. Other adjectives are also used as adverbs without any change at all; among these we may list the words *little, less, least, long, better, best, worse, worst, much, more,* and *enough*. For the grammarian, these words represent only some of the more elementary difficulties that obscure the distinctions between adjectives and adverbs.

Nevertheless, your own errors will probably result from the simple omissions of the *-ly* or from confusion about certain common adjectives and the corresponding adverbs that do not take the *-ly* ending. In all doubtful cases, check your dictionary.

ORIGINAL

He plays baseball *real good.*

I spend *considerable* more than I make.

She *sure* knows how to paint.

REVISION

He plays baseball *really well.*

I spend *considerably* more than I make.

She *certainly* knows how to paint. (The colloquial *sure* is sometimes acceptable—and better, in our opinion, than the stilted *surely. Certainly* is more appropriate than either in most expository writing.)

(See **Adjective.**)

---

agr/pa   **Agreement/Pronoun-Antecedent**—Make each pronoun agree with its antecedent.

A pronoun agrees with its antecedent (the word it refers back to) in person, number, and gender.

I broke *my* toe playing football. (*My* is first person singular; it refers back to *I.*)

During the break between semesters, *we* went to *our* cabin in the Sierras. (*Our* is first person plural; it refers back to *we.*)

You should write *your* paper as soon as possible. (*Your* is second person; it may be either singular or plural. Here it is singular, referring back to *you,* which is also singular in this context.)

Jim and *Jan* have finally set *their* departure date. *(Their* is third person plural; it refers back to *Jim* and *Jan.)*

The used-car *salesman* swore by *his* mother's love that the Edsel was the best car ever made. *(His* is third person singular; it refers back to *salesman.)*

Martha St. John sadly sipped *her* Pernod and wondered if Paris was all it was supposed to be. *(Her* is third person singular; it refers back to *Martha St. John.* Obviously, *her* is of female gender, while *his,* of course, is masculine. Note that pronouns such as *I, you, we,* and *they* have no gender—that is, they refer to both sexes, or to either.)

Note Carefully: *in standard public prose do not use a singular pronoun to refer to a plural antecedent, or a plural pronoun to refer to a singular antecedent.*

Note in particular that words like *each, every, either, anybody, anyone, somebody, someone, everyone, neither, nobody* and *no one* **are always followed by singular pronouns.**

A special problem, however, is posed by the new awareness of that language which tends to place women in subordinate positions. Traditionally, it would be quite correct to use *his* to refer to both men and women, as in *"Each student* [singular] should pass *his* [masculine singular] paper forward." It's easier to say, *"Each student* should pass *their* [plural] paper forward," but the pronoun does not agree with its singular antecedent. (In some cases you might use the plural consistently: *"All students* should pass *their* papers forward.") Until some new convention develops, it is perhaps best to use the cumbersome "his or her" construction, *depending on the circumstances.* As George Orwell advised, break any of the rules of grammar and style rather than say something barbarous.

ORIGINAL

Every boy in the whole world loves *their* dog, even if *they* are mangy *beasts. (Every boy* and *dog* are singular; the pronouns that follow should be singular.)

Everyone sat on *their* hands when the group paused for the expected cheers. *(Everyone* is singular; the pronoun that follows *should* be singular, but, as we noted above, the more formal *his* represents gender discrimination.)

(See **Reference.**)

REVISION

Every boy in the whole world loves *his* dog, even if *it* is a mangy beast.

Everyone sat on *his* hands when the group paused for the expected cheers.

---

agr / sv   **Agreement/Subject-Verb**—Make each verb agree with its subject.

1. A singular subject requires a singular verb; a plural subject requires a plural verb:

> Ice *is* usually hard, clear, and cold. (The singular subject *ice* takes the singular verb *is.*)

> The books *are* on the table. (The plural subject *books* takes the plural verb *are.*)

Exceptions

(a) A plural subject that names either an extent or a quantity taken as a unit requires a singular verb.

> Twenty miles *is* a long walk for anyone. (The plural subject *miles,* taken as a unit, requires a singular verb, *is.*)

> Seven dollars *is* too much to pay for this room, in my opinion. (The plural subject *dollars,* taken as a unit, requires a singular verb, *is.*)

(b) A singular subject that refers to the members of a group requires a plural verb—when the members are considered to be acting individually.

> The class *are* in their seats now. (The singular subject *class* takes the plural verb *are*—and the plural pronoun *their*—because the members are represented as acting individually.)

2. Two or more subjects joined by *and* usually take a plural verb:

> *Through the Looking Glass* and *Alice in Wonderland are* two of my favorite books.

> Witchcraft, idolatry, and blasphemy *were* capital crimes in the Massachusetts Bay Colony.

Exceptions

(a) When the subjects joined by *and* refer to the same person, or when they name things thought of as a logical unit, the verb is singular.

> My guide and interpreter *is* a lovely young girl who goes by the name of Lisa.

> This bread and cheese *is* a meal in itself.

(b) When the subjects joined by *and* are preceded by *each* or *every*, the verb is singular.

> Each wheel and each gear *is* carefully inspected by an expert.

3. Subjects joined by *or, nor, either . . . or, neither . . . nor* may take a singular or plural verb:

(a) When both subjects are singular, the verb is singular:

> Neither Jonathan nor Omar *is going* to share my dinner.

(b) When both subjects are plural, the verb is plural:

> Since neither the administrators nor the students *were willing* to compromise, the love-in became a riot.

(c) When one subject is singular and the other is plural, the verb agrees with the nearer subject:

> Neither the President nor his advisors fully *understand* the problems of the urban poor.

> No spices or flavoring *is* used in this recipe.

> Neither you nor she *is* entirely wrong.

4. The indefinite pronouns *each, either, neither, anybody, anyone, everyone, everybody, someone, somebody, no one, nobody,* and *one* always take a singular verb:

> Each one of us *is* waiting his time.

> Nobody *knows* the trouble I've seen.

5. The relative pronouns *who, which,* and *that* are singular if the antecedent is singular, and plural if the antecedent is plural:

> Cats that *fight* dogs don't live long. *(That* is plural, and it takes a plural verb.)

> A cat that *fights* dogs won't live long. *(That* is singular, and it takes a singular verb.)

> He is the sort of man who *dreams* of beautiful and profligate girls while calmly discussing the budget with his wife. *(Who* is singular, and it takes a singular verb.)

> He is a man who *builds* roads and tunnels that *lead* nowhere. (*Who* is singular and it takes a singular verb. *That* is plural, and it takes a plural verb.)

Problems in Subject-Verb Agreement

1. Do not be confused by words or phrases that separate the subject from its verb:

ORIGINAL

The *reason* for the impoverished condition of my finances *are* rather embarrassing. (The singular subject, *reason*, should have a singular verb, *is*, not the plural verb *are*. *For the impoverished condition of my finances* merely modifies the subject without influencing the verb in any way.)

REVISION

The *reason* for the impoverished condition of my finances *is* rather embarrassing.

2. Do not be confused by sentences beginning *there is* or *there are*; in such sentences, the subject with its modifiers, if any, follows the verb:

ORIGINAL

There *is* troubled times ahead. (The plural subject, *times*, requires a plural verb, *are*, not the singular verb *is*.)

REVISION

There *are* troubled times ahead.

3. Do not be confused by words that are plural in form but singular in meaning—for instance, *civics, economics, genetics, linguistics, mathematics, news, physics, semantics*. Such words take a singular verb:

By showing us how language works, *semantics helps* us to understand ourselves and other people. (The singular subject *semantics* takes a singular verb, *helps*.)

A few words that are always plural in form may be either singular or plural in meaning, depending on how they are used: *politics* and *statistics*, for instance, are sometimes singular and sometimes plural. Consult a good college desk dictionary to distinguish the various meanings of these words.

ap

Apostrophe—Use apostrophes to show possession; to make plurals of numbers, letters, and symbols; and to show omissions in contracted words or numbers.

1. *Possession.* Show possession by the addition of an apostrophe or an apostrophe and s. As a general rule, add only an apostrophe if the word already ends in s:

SINGULAR	PLURAL
the *girl's* dresses	the *girls'* dresses
the *boy's* books	the *boys'* books
Mr. *Johnson's* car	the *Johnsons'* cars
child's toys	*children's* toys

2. *Plural of numbers.* Form the plural of numbers by the addition of an apostrophe and s:

His 7's are hard to read.

Of all his guns, the 45's were the most deadly.

3. *Plural of letters.* Form the plural of letters by the addition of an apostrophe and s:

Too many *D's* spoiled Mike's grade average.

There are two o's in *too*.

4. *Plural of symbols.* Form the plural of symbols by the addition of an apostrophe and s:

The page was covered with + 's, = 's, and $'s.

5. *Plural of slang used as written words.* Form the plural of slang words by the addition of an apostrophe and s:

Her speech is filled with clichés: I heard at least seven *right on's*, five *far out's*, and four *wow's* in the time it took to walk down the steps and across the main parking lot.

6. *Contractions*. Form contractions by using an apostrophe in the place of missing letters or numbers:

The '65 Buicks were reliable cars.

It's not the heat that gets me; it's the humidity.

The old man isn't the tennis player he was a few years ago; I beat him two games today.

Do not use apostrophes with the possessive pronouns *his, hers, its, ours, yours, theirs, whose.*

WRONG

Here's my car, but where's your's?

RIGHT

Here's my car, but where's yours?

Never use an apostrophe simply to form a plural.

WRONG

The Mittrick's live here.

RIGHT

The Mittricks live here.

aud

Audience—Write for a general audience unless otherwise instructed.

Who reads your papers? You believe with some certainty that your papers are likely to be read only by your instructors, who know what you have read and discussed, what has happened in class, and what the assignment is. Nevertheless, you should write for a *general audience* in most expository papers. The general audience is "out there": *not* your instructors, *not* a fellow student, but someone who might find your paper on a street corner, someone who knows nothing of your classroom work. This particular someone should be thought of as your audience, the *general audience* for whom you are writing. The general audience should be considered informed, literate, and worthy of your respect. The situation is artificial at this point, but remember that in later life, when you write expository prose, you will most likely be writing for a general audience.

Remember, then:

1. *Orient your audience.* Fill in background information, since you cannot assume that your audience knows anything about your writing assignment. For instance, suppose that you are writing about Hemingway's story "A Clean, Well-Lighted Place." Identify the author and title; briefly sum up the plot; then state your thesis:

> In his story "A Clean, Well-Lighted Place," Ernest Hemingway presents three main characters: an old man who likes to drink late at a cafe, the "clean, well-lighted place"; a younger waiter who is anxious to get home to his wife; and an older waiter who is in no hurry because he identifies with those who need a light for the night and because he knows he will not sleep until dawn. The story presents the older waiter's deeply moving confrontation with *nada,* the existential Nothingness that characterizes his universe, and by implication, the world in which many men and women live.

2. *Write in an appropriate style.* For a general audience, you should avoid extremely colloquial prose on the one hand and excessively formal prose on the other. That means, in effect, that you should write *Standard Editorial English* (see **Sentence Structure/Style** and **Usage**). Colloquial prose is characterized by loose sentence structure and word choices more appropriate to speech than to expository writing. Excessively formal prose is marked by disproportionate use of longer, more involved sentences and highly Latinate diction.

awk, k

Awkward Phrasing—Phrase each sentence as clearly and forcefully as possible. Revise any wording that seems awkward, clumsy, inept, vague, or ambiguous. Use exact words arranged simply and clearly.

ORIGINAL

The conformist type of parent does not delve into the origin on why he should raise a family or see the great value that consummates in raising a family. In his hands he has a child that he can mold the mind to search or let the child be raised in our ethics and mores of society to be mediocre. The asset of having a parent who will encourage a child to think is worth more than 500 parents who are consistently wanting to do the same as his neighbors. (This is confused, ugly, and verbose. The student has an idea but cannot express it: such prose is painful to read and probably more painful to write.)

REVISION

The parent who merely conforms does not see any great value in raising a family. He doesn't realize that he has a *choice:* he can either let his children grow up believing in the traditional mores of our society, or he can mold their minds to search for individual ideas. A parent who can encourage his children to think is worth five hundred parents who consistently want them to do as their neighbors do. (This is simpler and clearer. But because this passage can now be *read,* the student who wrote it should be able to see that he needs to examine his ideas with some care. In sentence one, for instance, he should see that the word *value* demands some explanation. What value? Who receives it—the parent, the children, society in general? Or is *value* perhaps the wrong word here? The answers to these questions should lead to further rewriting and greater clarity.)

Awkward phrasing comes in such bewildering variety that any attempt at classification is simply futile. But we can often show *why* a given phrase is awkward.

1. A phrase may be awkward because the writer has chosen the wrong word:

ORIGINAL

His most undesirable attribute is that he is *perverted* to killing people, fighting, and other acts of violence. (He may indeed be perverted, but the use of the word in this construction leads to a series of clumsy phrases where three short verbs would serve better.)

REVISION

His most undesirable attribute is that he kills, fights, and commits other violent acts.

2. A phrase may be awkward because the writer has used indirect, wordy constructions:

ORIGINAL

By "other-directed" *it is meant* not to be bound by habits, traditions, or prejudices. *("By . . . it is meant"* is an impersonal construction; it forces the writer to use too many words. See **Impersonal Construction.**)

REVISION

Other-directed means "not bound by habits, traditions, or prejudices."

3. Awkward phrasing may be simply verbal clutter:

ORIGINAL

Unfortunately, any experience I had that was at all useful (in bringing in an income) was in the class of being either non-paying or highly professional, and things like motorcycle-racing, scuba-diving, or cat-burgling fell into this vast collection. (This writer uses too many words but has a fine sense of humor. He could be saved.)

REVISION

Unfortunately, any useful experience I had was either unsalaried or highly professional, like motorcycle-racing, scuba-diving, or cat-burgling.

What should you do, then, about revising your own awkward phrasing? Our best advice is to use your dictionary, first of all, and to cut out all unnecessary words. *Be clear, simple, and direct.*

(See **Sentence Structure/Style, Impersonal Construction, Passive Construction,** and **Wrong Word.**)

b

br

Brackets—Use brackets within a direct quotation to enclose an explanation, a correction, or a comment.

> "Another reason for this exaggerated enthusiasm [for translations] is that our current poets are at a loss as to what to write. Translation is a way to get a poem without having to go into it for yourself."
>
> —Gene Fowler, "The Poet as Translator"
> (*Trace*, No. 12, 1968–69, p. 372)

A special kind of comment often enclosed in brackets is the editorial remark *sic,* a Latin word meaning "thus." Use *sic,* enclosed in brackets, to indicate that you are reproducing a word or phrase exactly as it was written.

> In his report on his progress at school, Mike wrote: "My principle [*sic*] feels that my spelling needs work whereas my atheletic [*sic*] abilities do not."

(See **Parentheses.**)

C

---

cap

Capital Letters—Use capital letters where they are required by the conventions of the written language.

Every written language has its own peculiar rules governing the use of capital letters—rules hardened by tradition and not to be broken by logic. The rules for American English are set down here. Unless you are already famous for your iconoclastic style, you had better learn them.

1. Capitalize proper nouns and proper adjectives (nouns and adjectives that distinguish an individual person, place, or thing from others of the same class):

> Her name is Joan.

> In England, I drank German beer, ate French food, and went to Swedish movies.

2. Capitalize the names of races, peoples, tribes, and languages:

> He's a Cherokee Indian, but he speaks Japanese like a native.

3. Capitalize the first words of a sentence or an expression standing for a sentence:

"Did you see that?"

"Wow!"

"Heavy stuff, man."

4. Capitalize the first word of each line of traditional verse:

Western wind, when will thou blow,
The small rain down can rain?
Christ, if my love were in my arms
And I in my bed again!

5. Capitalize the first word of a direct quotation:

But the gentleman dressed in white paper
leaned forwards and whispered in her ear,
"Never mind what they say, my dear, but take
a return-ticket every time the train stops."

—Lewis Carroll, *Through the Looking-Glass*

6. Capitalize all references to the Deity:

"In the name of the Father, and of the Son,
and of the Holy Ghost, amen."

7. Capitalize days of the week, the names of months, holy days, holidays, and festivals:

On Saturday, December 25, we will celebrate
Christmas as usual—with too many toys and
too much food.

8. Capitalize titles when they appear before the name of the bearer:

I shook hands with President Tyler and
Senator Scott.

9. Capitalize the first word—and each of the other words except unemphatic articles, conjunctions, and prepositions—in the titles of plays, magazines,

poems, movies, stories, essays, and musical selections. As a general rule, the articles (the words *the, a,* and *an)* are always unemphatic; prepositions and conjunctions fewer than six letters long are usually unemphatic.

> Have you read *Oh, Dad, Poor Dad, Mama's Hung You in the Closet and I'm Feelin' So Sad?*

10. Capitalize North, East, South, and West, and their combined forms (Middle West, Southwest), when they refer to a specific geographic section of the country. (But do not capitalize such words when they refer merely to direction.)

> "I'm from the South," she said proudly.

> We drove north for two hours.

11. Capitalize brand names and registered trademarks:

> She was wearing tight, faded Levi's and drinking a Coke; from her Keds to her Toni she was one hundred percent American.

Avoid unnecessary capitals.

WRONG	RIGHT
I am taking Geography and History.	I am taking geography and history.
	I am taking Geography 1a and History 17b.
Of course I love my Mother.	Of course I love my mother. Of course I love Mother. (In this sentence *Mother* is a proper noun and should be capitalized.)

(See **Lower-Case Letters.**)

case

Case (of pronouns)—Use the correct case for each pronoun construction.

Case, grammatically, designates the ending of a word, or a new form of a word, used to show how that word is related to other words in context.

Highly inflected languages, like Latin, use cases extensively to show grammatical relationships. For example,"Canis hominem momordit" means "The dog bit the man." But "Canem homo momordit" means "The man bit the dog." In other words, case shows *who* did *what* to *whom*.

In English, fortunately, only pronouns have a complicated system of cases. As a speaker of the language, you *know* all of these cases, and listing them here would be pointless.

Let us concentrate instead on two principles: first, use the *subject case* of pronouns for the subjects of verbs and the complements of linking verbs; secondly, use the *object case* of pronouns for the objects of verbs and prepositions.

SUBJECT CASE

(who, whoever)

Who loves me?

I know *who* loves me.

Whoever did it will suffer.

I will punish *whoever* did it.

(Who is the subject of *loves; whoever* is the subject of *did.)*

OBJECT CASE

(Whom, whomever)

Whom do I love?

I know *whom* I love.

Choose *whomever* you want.

I will punish *whomever* I find guilty.

(Whom is the object of *love* in both sentences; *whomever* is the object of *want* in the third sentence, and the object of *find* in the last sentence.)

Exceptions

Idiomatic speech and informal writing allow us

great freedom in using the subject case where the object case is formally required.

Who did you see last night?

Who did you give my message to?

are both grammatically incorrect, for example. But in each sentence the use of *whom* would have sounded stilted.

SUBJECT CASE

(*I, we, he/she, they* as subjects)

I said, "Hah! You're a dirty old man!"

She and *I* sat on my roof one night, and *we* talked until the sun came up.

He agrees that the only solution to the problem will be unacceptable to our parents.

They stood just outside my window.

(*I, we, he/she,* and *they* all serve as subjects.)

OBJECT CASE

(*me, us, him/her, them* as objects)

The sun hit *us* just right.

She taught *me* a lesson.

I saw *him* with another woman, and if I know *her*, he's in bad trouble.

Do you see *them*?

(*Me, us, him/her,* and *them* all serve as direct objects of verbs.)

SUBJECT CASE

(*I, we, he/she, they* as complements)

It is *I* that I want to talk about.

It was *they* and *we* who lost all our savings.

I thought it was *he* and *she* I saw together.

But it seems to be *they* who should go.

(*I, we, he, she,* and *they* are complements of linking verbs.)

OBJECT CASE

(*me, us, him/her, them* as objects of prepositions)

She gave 10,000 kisses to *me* that lovely night.

In *us* there was perfect harmony; in *them,* none.

His wife said to *him* and to *her,* "Just what the hell is going on here?"

Then she stepped on *them* both.

(*Me, us, him, her,* and *them* are objects of prepositions.)

Exceptions

Again, speech and informal writing permit us great freedom in the use of personal pronouns. "It is *I*" sounds stilted. Say, "It's *me*"—and don't feel guilty about using an object case after a linking verb.

Typical Errors in Pronoun Case:

ERROR

CORRECTION

But I was also interested in why the magazine was popular and to *who* it was most appealing. *(Who cannot serve as the object of the preposition to; whom therefore is required.)*

But I was also interested in why the magazine was popular and to *whom* it was most appealing.

Whomever it was, I was angry. *(Whomever cannot serve as the complement of the linking verb is.)*

Whoever it was, I was angry.

Whom shall I say is calling? *(Whom cannot serve as the subject of is calling; do not be confused by the intervening clause shall I say.)*

Who shall I say is calling?

Jerry and *me* went fishing. *(Me cannot serve as part of the subject of the verb went.)*

Jerry and *I* went fishing.

The fish were not biting for Jerry and *I*. *(I cannot serve as the object of the preposition for; do not be confused by the fact that Jerry is also the object of the preposition.)*

The fish were not biting for Jerry and *me*.

Us boys down at the brewery get all the free beer we can drink. *(Us, with boys, is a subject; hence you must say we boys.)*

We boys down at the brewery get all the free beer we can drink.

To *we* girls marriage is no longer very important. *(We, along with girls, is the object of the preposition to; hence you must say us girls.)*

To *us* girls marriage is no longer very important.

cl

Cliché—Use clichés and other extremely popular and fashionable expressions only when necessary or effective.

A cliché, specifically, is an over-used figure of speech: *that's the way the ball bounces; dead as a doornail; high as a kite; deadly as sin; as cool as a cucumber; a dog-eat-dog world.* Besides such similes and metaphors, however, the term *cliché* also refers to worn and ragged expressions of all sorts, many of which have lost their original meaning; *toe the line,* for example, originally meant to stand with one's toes touching a line as a starting point for a contest, but the phrase is so little understood now that it is often written *tow the line.* (And our students keep telling us it's a *doggy-dog* world.) Hence any extremely popular or fashionable phrase may be considered a cliché: stock expressions ("last but not least"); quotations ("To be or not to be . . ."); foreign expressions *("bête noire," "c'est la vie," "che sera sera");* and slogans of the hour and the latest catch-words *("Right on!" "Far out!").*

Every writer is tempted by clichés: a ready-made phrase is a ready-made thought. Not thinking eliminates *some* of the work of writing. The good writer, however, does his own thinking and his own phrase-making, although at times a cliché *may* be appropriate and effective. For example: "She was as ugly as sin—but just as much fun!"

Be alert to clichés. They stalk you at every twist of the pen. Scratch your head and one pops up. To cure yourself of a habit as nasty (for a writer) as nose-picking, try writing a paragraph packed with clichés like this one:

Why I Want a College Education

In the fast-moving world of today in which we live, the man who wants to go places in a big hurry needs that old sheepskin. Education is important if you're going to get a good job. Once you leave the nest you have to land on your feet and start running just to keep your head above the tide in the fast-moving world of today. Without a college diploma you will wind up on the streets along with the rest of the unemployed and the economically deprived, since every day it's harder to get a good job without a college education. In this world life is not just a bowl of cherries, it's a dog-eat-dog battle for survival, best man win, winner take all. You've got to get in there and fight, hammer and tongs, tooth and nail, to win out over your worthy opponent. If you need to climb the ladder of success on other men's dead bodies, do it. But you can't sit back and wait for all the goodies to be handed to you on a golden platter—unless you were born with a silver spoon in your mouth. Every individual is in competition with every other individual in our complex, fast-moving world of today, with its rapidly advancing technology. To beat the other man you need a college education. That's why I'm going to college. And may the best man win!

C:

Colon—Use the colon[:], following a main clause, to introduce a list, an explanation, or a formal quotation, and in certain other constructions.

1. List:

   Everywhere you look in Paris there are signs of American influence: American cars, American soft drinks, American cigarettes, American dollars.

2. Explanation:

>   I began to doubt Martha's love: surely the arsenic in my coffee was no accident.

3. Formal Quotation:

>   In Rex Stout's series of mystery stories, Archie Goodwin and Inspector Cramer delight in badgering one another. Here, for instance, Archie has just insulted Cramer:
>
>>   His face, chronically red, deepened a shade. His broad shoulders stiffened, and the creases spreading from the corners of his gray-blue eyes showed more as the eyelids tightened. Then, deciding I was playing for a blurt, he controlled it. "Do you know," he asked, "whose opinion of you I would like to have? Darwin's. Where were you while evolution was going on?"

Do not use a colon in the middle of a clause; use the colon only at the end of a clause.

ORIGINAL

At the party there were: John Dykes, Vickie Meade, April Archer, and Dorian Flick. (Here the colon is used, incorrectly, in the middle of a clause.)

REVISION

At the party there were John Dykes, Vickie Meade, April Archer, and Dorian Flick.

The following people were at the party: John Dykes, Vickie Meade, April Archer, and Dorian Flick.

4. Use the colon between chapter and verse in references to the Bible:

>   Genesis 9: 3–8
>
>   John 3: 1–4

5. Use the colon between hours and minutes in indicating time:

>   It is now 4:05 P.M.
>
>   I got up at 5:00 A.M.

Always place the colon outside quotation marks:

> I have just read Gene Fowler's comments on his story "Felon's Journal": the piece is so deft and subtle that I felt I needed some guidance on the author's aims.

---

c

Comma—Use a comma where the structure of a sentence demands one.

The comma marks a very slight pause in the flow of a sentence. In speech, such a pause usually follows a rise in the pitch of the voice; that is, the voice actually reaches a higher tone just before the pause. Consequently, if you can "hear" your own writing—and if you remember that writing is a reflection of the spoken language—you will be able to use your natural good judgment in placing commas.

You should also consult the following rules:

1. Use a comma to separate words, phrases, and clauses in a series:

Words

Mephisto (my black cat) eats only *beef kidney, chicken hearts, creamed corn,* and *raw mice.*

Phrases

At the same party, Martha St. John *climbed to the top of the stairs, removed her glass eye, jumped for the chandelier,* and *swung upside down by her legs,* while reciting a poem about Tarzan and apes.

Clauses

Then she ran into the bedroom, she threw herself onto the bed, and *she burst out into tears and choking sobs.*

Exception

The final comma is sometimes omitted in a brief, clear series:

His poems are simple, clear and deeply moving.

But the omission is not particularly daring or modern; it obscures the relationship between the spoken sounds and the written words; and it may be confusing. If you want to be clear, courteous, and exact—instead of stubborn, boorish, and arch—you will leave the final comma where it belongs: in the series.

2. Use a comma to separate coordinate adjectives (adjectives of equal rank and importance):

a *tender, succulent* steak

a *beautiful, gentle, sweet* girl

To apply a simple test for coordinate adjectives, you can change their order and insert the word *and* (as in *a succulent and tender steak*). If the meaning is still clear, the adjectives are coordinate.

When one adjective is considered part of the noun, however, the adjectives are not coordinate and should not be separated by a comma:

the *good old* days

Old days is a unit. Thus *good* and *old* are not coordinate. If they were, you could reverse the order and insert *and* without twisting the sense of the phrase. But *the good old days* does not mean *the old and good days*.

3. Use a comma before the conjunction in a compound sentence:

A compound sentence contains two main clauses—by definition, clauses that *could* stand alone as separate sentences. In a compound sentence, such clauses are usually—but not always—joined by a coordinating conjunction; a semicolon sometimes takes the place of the conjunction:

> Eda wanted oysters on the half-shell, *but* I wanted cherrystone clams.

> Eda wanted oysters on the half-shell; I wanted cherrystone clams.

The coordinating conjunctions in English are *and, or, nor, but, yet,* and *for.* Note that in the following compound sentences, commas are used before each of these conjunctions:

> Medical researchers have already created a vast variety of mood-controlling drugs, *and* even pills to increase intelligence seem to be within the realm of possibility.

> You go by yourself, *or* I'll go with you.

> I seldom drink to excess, *nor* do I use profanity.

> "Candy is dandy, *but* liquor is quicker."

> He loves fishing, *yet* he seldom has time for it.

> Donna was very tired, *for* she had missed a lot of sleep.

Exception

For a sharper break between the two clauses, a semicolon may be used even when the conjunction is retained:

> I begged her to come on Friday; *but* she had to work.

Caution: Do not confuse a compound sentence with a simple sentence containing a compound predicate—that is, a sentence containing a single subject but two or more verbs. Such a sentence should not have a comma before the conjunction.

ORIGINAL

The sun dropped slowly over the horizon, and fell into the sea. (The comma is not required because this is a simple sentence, containing a single subject with two verbs.)

REVISION

The sun dropped slowly over the horizon and fell into the sea.

4. Use comma punctuation to set off a non-restrictive word, phrase, or clause following a noun:

Nonrestrictive words, phrases, or clauses simply add more information. They are not essential to the meaning of the sentence—and could be dropped without changing the basic meaning.

Note how the comma is used with each of the following nonrestrictive constructions. Note, in addition, that the comma also *follows* the word, phrase, or clause when the construction is set in the middle of the sentence:

Word

Gregor Samsa, *salesman,* will appear on *The Johnny Carson Show* tonight.

Ernst, *my neighbor,* shoots pool and drinks bourbon almost every night.

Phrase

The sky, *darkening suddenly,* seemed to be afloat swiftly in scudding black clouds.

My money, *not being essential to her happiness,* surely was not a factor in her falling in love with me, was it?

Clause

I was very embarrassed when my girl, *who was only slightly drunk,* broke a heel and went crashing halfway down the stairs, as her glass hit the ceiling and a shower of champagne fell on the other guests.

Gene Fowler, *who happens to be a great poet,* is my best friend.

5. Use a comma to set off a long introductory phrase or subordinate clause:

Phrase

After waiting in the bar for two hours, we were hungry enough to eat braised buffalo liver au gratin.

On the night of the big game, twelve people turned out to welcome the team home.

Clause

Although he was perhaps America's greatest poet, Ezra Pound still spent twelve years in a federal insane asylum awaiting trial for treason allegedly committed during World War II.

While walking on the beach one day, I found a walrus eating oysters. [An *elliptical* clause: the subject and part of the verb—"I was"—are understood even though not directly expressed.]

6. Use a comma to set off a nonrestrictive subordinate clause at the end of a sentence; omit the comma if the clause is restrictive:

Nonrestrictive

I won't marry her, *even though she is young and beautiful.*

I wanted that car very much, *although I knew I could not possibly afford it.*

Restrictive

I wouldn't marry her *if she had a million dollars.*

We learned our lesson *after we spent just one night in jail.*

7. Use a comma after an introductory participial or gerund construction:

Participles are verbal adjectives. The present participle ends in -ing; the past participle ends in -ed when the verb is regular, but in irregular verbs its ending varies according to the custom of the language. Thus *walking* and *swimming* are forms of the present participle; *walked* and *swum* are forms of the past participle.

Gerunds are verbal *nouns*. Like present participles, gerunds end in -ing. To tell the difference between a gerund and a present participle, simply decide whether the word functions as a noun or an adjective. Unless you are especially interested in grammar, however, you probably will feel no compelling drive to discern the difference. Don't worry about it: the distinction is usually unimportant when it comes to this rule of comma punctuation.

Participial Constructions

Grabbing my can of insect-killer, I quickly slaughtered a silverfish. (*Grabbing* is a present participle.)

Having swum a mile, I began to tire. (*Having swum* is a past participle.)

Gerund Constructions

By killing just one silverfish, I benefit humanity and myself, perpetually at war with the insect population. (*Killing* is a gerund.)

After singing our quota of songs for the night, we boys from Camp Swampy sat around the campfire and told tall tales. (*Singing* is a gerund.)

8. A word, phrase, or clause that interrupts the sentence in any way should usually be set off by commas:

Word

And that, *my love,* is the story of my life.

It is, *however,* very difficult to hit a silverfish from more than ten feet away.

Phrase

That song, *in my opinion,* is inane and unimaginative.

Mike would be much improved, *on the contrary,* by a sudden impact with a moving train.

Clause

Dr. Johnson's *Dictionary, it seems to me,* makes very interesting reading.

The lights down below, *I think,* are very beautiful at this time of morning, when the sun is just beginning to rise out of the darkness and into layers of purple and pink sky.

9. Use a comma to separate a brief direct quotation from the rest of the sentence:

Jonathan Wild looked closely at her and said, "I think I could learn to like you."

"In fact," he added, "you're the most beautiful golden retriever I've ever seen."

10. Use a comma to set off words and phrases that mark a transition in thought at the beginning of a sentence:

However, he knew that Martha would never let him keep a dog.

Indeed, Martha hated dogs.

On the other hand, Martha was something of a beast herself, and. . . .

After all, a dog that beautiful would undoubtedly behave better than Martha, who insisted on taking out her glass eye at the most inappropriate moments and polishing it on her sleeve like a piece of costume jewelry.

11. Use a comma to set off numbers indicating thousands:

    10,000 $5,230,000

12. Use a comma to separate month and year in writing dates:

    April, 1969, was an important month for me.

    Today is March 5, 1976.

    On July 30, 1975, I left for London.

13. Use a comma to prevent confusion:

    For Elizabeth, Anne was a faithful friend and a charming companion.

    Just before, I had run into the rear bumper of a Redwood City police car.

    What shall be, shall be.

14. Always place the comma inside the quotation marks, unless the quotation itself is followed by a parenthesis:

    I have just finished reading "Flight," which is one of my favorite short stories.

    I have just finished reading "Flight" (you know, by John Steinbeck), which is one of my favorite short stories.

Despite this profusion of rules, we have severely *limited* our account of the circumstances under which commas should be used. We should now reiterate a point we made earlier: check the rules when you need to, but, for the most part, *rely on your common sense:* an inner ear will usually tell you when to use commas.

CS

Comma Splice—Do not write two main clauses joined by a comma.

This construction—a "comma splice"—is a gross mechanical error, in the minds of many instructors, because it suggests that the writer is unable to recognize basic sentence units. In other words, joining two complete sentences with *just* a comma is a violation of sacred rules, although many professional writers do it. It is a good idea, nevertheless, to break rules only when you can get away with doing so—in this case, outside the classroom, in fiction, poetry, letters, and in informal writing generally.

1. Correct some comma splices by using a coordinating conjunction with the comma:

COMMA SPLICE

He has completed his research, he will report his findings to the class today.

(See **Comma.**)

CORRECTION

He has completed his research, *and* he will report his findings to the class today.

2. Correct some comma splices by replacing the comma with a semicolon:

He has completed his research; he will report his findings to the class today.

(See **Semicolon.**)

3. Correct some comma splices by replacing the comma with a period:

> He has completed his research. He will report his findings to the class today.

4. Correct some comma splices by using a dash:

COMMA SPLICE

I like Julian Symon's novels, he always tells an exciting story.

(See **Dash.**)

CORRECTION

I like Julian Symon's novels—he always tells a good story.

5. Correct some comma splices by using a colon:

COMMA SPLICE

Everyone should have a telephone with an on-off switch, it gives him a tie with the outside world but allows him his privacy, too.

(See **Colon.**)

CORRECTION

Everyone should have a telephone with an on-off switch: it gives him a tie with the outside world but allows him his privacy, too.

Note: many comma splices result from elementary confusion about a class of words called *conjunctive adverbs*. These are words and phrases which, like conjunctions, *link* ideas but technically serve as *adverbs* (hence their name). Conjunctive adverbs in English include such terms as *then, first, secondly, however, nevertheless, for example, none the less, finally, furthermore, likewise, moreover, meanwhile, soon, hence, accordingly, therefore, thus,* and *consequently.* While the list is by no means complete, it does suggest some of the qualities of conjunctive adverbs: they link ideas together, they show relationships, they indicate comparison and contrast, they signal how one thing happens after or as a result of another thing: that is, they function as *directional signs in English. But they cannot be used to join clauses grammatically, as in the following comma-spliced sentences:*

I like soft rock, *however* I *also* like modern jazz.

He studied hard, *nevertheless* he didn't do well on the final exam.

Oedipus Rex is a very proud man, *thus* he often finds it hard to believe he could be mistaken or do any wrong, even inadvertently, *consequently* he believes that people like Teiresias and Kreon are plotting against him.

We drove seven hours to reach the mountains, *then* we spent the rest of the day skiing.

I tried and tried to fix my car, *finally* I called a garage.

Such sentences can be repaired in any of the ways listed above, or you may want to completely rewrite the sentence. Consider these corrections, for instance:

Semicolon

I like soft rock; *however,* I *also* like modern jazz. He studied hard; *nevertheless,* he didn't do well on the final exam.

Colon plus conjunction

Oedipus Rex is a proud man: *thus* he often finds it hard to believe he could be mistaken or do any wrong, even inadvertently, *and consequently* he believes that people like Teiresias and Kreon are plotting against him.

Period

We drove several hours to reach the mountains. *Then* we spent the rest of the day skiing.

Conjunction

I tried and tried to fix my car, *but finally* I called a garage.

The method you choose will depend on the sentences themselves and their context. If you have just written a short sentence, you may now want a longer one; if you have just written a long sentence, you may now want two shorter ones. You may want the unique rhythm—the half-break in the flow of a sentence—created by a semicolon. Don't correct the error mechanically: correct it with a sense of style.

---

conc

Conclusion—Conclude your essays; don't just stop writing them.

Use the conclusion as a convenient exit for both reader and writer, a way of stepping graciously out the door. The conclusion gives you a chance to draw inferences, assert the importance of your ideas, or summarize your basic points. Use that chance.

1. Concluding the paragraph:

Most paragraphs used as parts of essays have no "concluding" sentence. The reason for this is, of course, that these paragraphs lead on to something else in the essay. But the paragraph written as a short composition—the kind of paragraph you often write in college—usually does have a sentence that we can label "conclusion." There are no simple rules for such a sentence; you will have to be guided by your own good sense. We will simply remind you that at the end of any composition you have your final chance to impress your reader. Even in writing a "one-paragraph essay" you will probably want to use this opportunity. To do so, *end with a sentence that restates your main idea or draws a logical conclusion from the evidence you have presented.*

Consider one example of the effective conclusion in the paragraph. Here, Vance Packard begins with the following topic sentence: "The early nineteen fifties witnessed the beginnings of a revolution in American advertising: Madison Avenue became conscious of the *unconscious.*" In the concluding sentence he cleverly rephrases this idea by substituting *ad* for Madison Avenue and *id* (the source of our unconscious desires) for the *unconscious:* "The ad is being tailored to meet the needs of the id."

> The early nineteen fifties witnessed the beginning of a revolution in American advertising: Madison Avenue became conscious of the *unconscious.* Evidence had piled up that the responses of consumers to the questions of market researchers were frequently unreliable—in other words, that people often don't want what they say they want. Some years ago, for instance, a great automobile company committed one of the costliest blunders in automobile history through reliance on old-style "nose counting" methods. Direct consumer surveys indicated that people wanted a sensible car in tune with the times—without frills, maneuverable and easy to park. A glance at today's cars—elongated, fish-finned and in riotous technicolor—shows how misleading were the results of the survey. Errors of this sort

convinced manufacturers and advertisers that they must take into account the irrationality of consumer behavior—that they must carry their surveys into the submerged areas of the human mind. The result is a strange and rather exotic phenomenon entirely new to the market place—the use of a kind of mass psychoanalysis to guide campaigns of persuasion. The ad is being tailored to meet the needs of the id.

> —Vance Packard, "The Ad and the Id"
> (*Harper's Bazaar,* August 1967, p. 97)

2. Concluding the essay:

The last paragraph of your essay should drive home your main points by summarizing or repeating your thesis. *And under no circumstances should you introduce a new idea in the last paragraph,* for, naturally, your reader would expect further development of such a point.

To get into the final paragraph, use appropriate transitional words: *then, finally, thus, in short, therefore* (but not *in conclusion,* which should be reserved for longer works.) For instance, in the following paragraph, Robert M. Hutchins concludes his comments on an ideal (Utopian) educational system by writing:

> *Thus* the educational system of Utopia [an ideal world] is a paradigm, or prototype, or model of the republic of learning and the world political republic for which the Utopians yearn. The civilization that the Utopians have established is one in which discussion takes the place of force, and consensus is the basis of action. In theoretical matters the Utopians believe that the

continuous refinement of methods and ideas will lead to the development of new ideas and hence to the advancement of knowledge. The Utopians are willing to examine the pretensions of any plan of action or of any theoretical proposition.

—Robert M. Hutchins, "Philosophical Diversity," *The University of Utopia* (Chicago: University of Chicago Press, 1953)

While we recommend, and some instructors require, a transitional expression early in the final paragraph of expository essays written for college classes, the professional may use subtler devices, while *implying* a transitional word. For instance, here is the final paragraph from Russell Lynes' "Highbrow, Lowbrow, Middlebrow." His thesis is that it isn't wealth or family that makes prestige these days: it's high thinking. He begins and ends his essay with a reference to his grandmother. The implied transitional word is *thus:*

If life for grandmother, who wouldn't dine with the Cartiers, was simple in its social distinctions, life is becoming equally simple for us. The rungs of the ladder may be different, it may even be a different ladder, but it's onward and upward just the same. You may not be known by which fork you use for the fish these days, but you will be known by which key you use for your *Finnegan's Wake.*

—Russell Lynes, "Highbrow, Lowbrow, Middlebrow," *The Tastemakers* (New York: Harper & Row, 1927)

Finally, here is a concluding paragraph from Robert Benchley's "Throwing Back the European Offensive." His transitional phrase, *whichever way,* refers back to the two methods he has recommended to combat the menace of returning travelers.

> Whichever way you pick to defend yourself against the assaults of people who want to tell you about Europe, don't forget that it was I who told you how. I'm going to Europe myself next year and if you try to pull either of these systems on *me* when I get back, I will recognize them at once, and it will just go all the harder with you. But of course, *I* will have something to tell that will be worth hearing.
>
> —*The Early Worm* (New York: Harper & Row, 1927).

con

Continuity—Write so that your ideas flow logically from sentence to sentence and from paragraph to paragraph—that is, give your writing continuity.

Continuity means literally "holding together." It's what gives your writing a sense of smoothness as you go from one idea to the next. You get continuity *first* by good organization, because the clear, logical arrangement makes the order of thought easy to follow.

(See **Organization.**)

You get continuity *secondly* from the language you use to tell your reader how your ideas fit together—you get it in transitions (connecting words and phrases).

(See **Transitions.**)

d

dm

Dangling Modifiers—Do not write sentences containing dangling modifiers.

Modifiers—almost always verbal phrases, in this case—are said to "dangle" when they fail to relate sensibly to the subject of the sentence: that is, they fail to modify the noun or pronoun that immediately follows the phrase, so that the sense of the sentence goes askew. For example, one student writes, *"Besides lying on the beach,* my time will be occupied in other constructive ways." Now, that sentence *says,* "My time was lying on the beach." Obviously the logic is twisted. The student *means,* "I will be lying on the beach"; hence he should have written, *"Besides lying on the beach,* I will spend my time in other constructive ways." Now the modifier no longer dangles. It hangs there just where it belongs: in front of the word *I.*

1. Correct some dangling modifiers by changing the main clause so that the modifier does, in fact, modify the subject.

DANGLING MODIFIER

With more exposure of their legs, men start to take more than casual glances at women. (The *men* are exposing their own legs?)

Having spent the day watching football games on television, my mother was furious with my father. (Your *mother* was watching football games?)

CORRECTION

With more exposure of their legs, women start to receive more than casual glances from men.

Having spent the day watching football games on television, my father suddenly found out that my mother was furious with him.

2. Correct some dangling modifiers by expanding the phrase into a subordinate clause:

DANGLING MODIFIER

While typing, my dog began to lick my toes. (The dog was *typing,* too?)

Flying at 20,000 feet, the cars looked like toys. (The cars were flying maybe, but not at 20,000 feet.)

To write poetry well, words need to be used imaginatively. (The *words* write the poems?)

CORRECTION

While I was typing, my dog began to lick my toes.

When we were flying at 20,000 feet, the cars looked like toys.

If you want to write poetry well, your words need to be used imaginatively. (This sentence is still awkward, but the modifier no longer dangles.)

---

d--

Dash—Use a dash (typed as two unspaced hyphens) to set off a sharp turn of thought within the sentence; to emphasize a parenthetical expression; and to set off parenthetical or appositional material introduced by certain expressions.

1. To set off a sharp turn of thought within the sentence:

I kissed her passionately and found—good grief!—that none of her teeth were hers.

2. To emphasize a parenthetical expression:

> Early morning—just as the birds waken and the black night turns dark shades of purple—is my favorite time of all.

3. To set off parenthetical or appositional material introduced by certain expressions *(namely, for example, that is, for instance,* etc.):

> I want two things out of life—*namely,* money and happiness.

> Right now his romantic life is extremely complicated—*that is,* he has two dates for Saturday night.

> Some automobiles were simply not built to hold up—*for example,* my Hupmobile.

Note: Dashes emphasize; parentheses de-emphasize; commas simply enclose. Use dashes discreetly.

Note also that dashes always go outside quotation marks:

> "Summer Is Icumen In"—an anonymous fifteenth-century lyric—is a playful evocation of the joys of spring and summer.

---

dev

Development—Develop each paragraph fully and completely.

Except for a few extremely brief paragraphs, used mainly for transition or for emphasis of a significant point, each paragraph should be developed in adequate detail. The following *methods of development* are most commonly used.

1. Develop some paragraphs by descriptive details:

> It was amusing to look around the *filthy little scullery* and think that only a *double door*

was between us and the *dining-room*. There
sat the *customers* in all their *splendour*—
spotless tablecloths, bowls of flowers, mirrors,
and *gilt cornices* and *painted cherubim;* and
here, just a *few feet away,* we in our *disgusting
filth. For it really was disgusting filth.* There
was no time to sweep the *floor* till evening,
and we slithered about in a compound of *soapy
water, lettuce-leaves, torn paper* and *trampled
food.* A *dozen waiters* with their *coats* off,
showing their *sweaty armpits,* sat at the *table*
mixing *salads* and sticking *their thumbs* into
the *cream pots.* The *room* had a *dirty, mixed
smell of food* and *sweat.* Everywhere in the
cupboards, behind the *piles* of *crockery,* were
squalid stores of food that the *waiters* had
stolen. There were only *two sinks,* and *no
washing basin,* and it was nothing unusual for
a *waiter* to wash his *face* in the *water* in
which *clean crockery* was rinsing. But the
customers saw nothing of this. There were a
coco-nut mat and a *mirror* outside the *dining-
room door,* and the *waiters* used to preen
themselves up and go in looking the *picture*
of cleanliness.

—George Orwell, *Down and Out in Paris and
London* (New York: Pocket Books, 1954, p. 78)

Although his style is quite different, Tom
Wolfe—a leading figure among the American "new
journalists"—also uses vivid descriptive techniques
in the following paragraph; Wolfe's writing, like
Orwell's, is so graphic one can almost *see* the
figures he describes:

The wheeps, beeps, freeps, electronic lulus,
Boomerang Modern and Flash Gordon
sunbursts soar on through the night over the
billowing hernia-hernia sounds and the old
babes at the slots—until it is 7:30 A.M. and I
am watching five men at a green-topped card

table playing poker. They are sliding their
Bee-brand cards into their hands and
squinting at the pips with a set to the lips like
Conrad Veidt in a tunic collar studying a code
message from S.S. headquarters. Big Sid
Wyman, the old Big-Time gambler from Saint
Louis, is there with his eyes looking like two
poached eggs engraved with a road map of
West Virginia after all night at the poker
table. Sixty-year-old Chicago Tommy Hargan
is there with his topknot of white hair pulled
back over his little pink skull and a mountain
of chips in front of his old caved-in sternum.
Sixty-two-year-old Dallas Maxie Welch is
there, fat and phlegmatic as an Indian Ocean
potentate. Two Los Angeles biggies are there
exhaling smoke from candella-green cigars
into the gloom. It looks like the perfect
vignette of every Big Time back room,
"athletic club," snooker house and floating
poker game in the history of the guys-and-
dolls lumpen-bourgeoisie. . . .

—Tom Wolfe, "Las Vegas (What?) Las Vegas
(Can't Hear You! Too Noisy) Las Vegas!!!!" *The
Kandy Colored Tangerine Flake Streamline
Baby* (New York: Farrar, Straus & Giroux, 1963)

2. Develop some paragraphs by facts and statistics:

Dr. Henry W. Turkel, the San Francisco
Coroner, conducted an investigation that should
have made many local doctors feel miserably
incompetent. In 100 cases he undertook
postmortem investigations and found
that the cause of death ascribed by the
attending physician was wrong nearly half the
time. Then he went on to a larger series of 400
cases. From these he selected 232 deaths in
which he ordinarily would have accepted the
evidence of the dead person's known history

or illness and the external examination of the body. Instead, Coroner Turkel treated these 232 deaths as if he had some reason to suspect the given cause. The careful post-mortems on each of these 232 deaths brought forth the fact that at least eight of them were due to some kind of hidden violence. Eight out of 232 means that 3.4 percent of all normally unsuspicious deaths might well be due to murder. In any given year this could easily be more than 25,000 perfect murders, or three times the known murders. In short, not only are most murders never solved, but there's a strong suspicion most murders are never detected.

—Murray Teigh Bloom, "Hows and Whys of the Perfect Murder" (*Playboy,* May 1965, p. 117)

3. Develop some paragraphs by multiple examples:

Among university scholars, a fad for toasting women in "some nauseous decoction" paralleled our latter-day panty raids and goldfish swallowing. In describing the drinking custom of 17th Century Oxford, one disapproving clergyman tells of a student who drank his mistress' health in wine mixed with a large spoonful of soot. "His companion, determined not to be outdone, brought from his closet a phial of ink, which he drank, exclaiming, 'To triumphe and Miss Molly!' " According to the same source, these "crack-brained young men also esteemed it a great privilege to get possession of a great beauty's shoe, in order that they might ladle wine out of a bowl down their throats with it, while they drank to the 'lady of little worth' or the 'light-heeled mistress' who had been its former wearer."

—William Iverson, "A Short History of Toasts and Toasting" (*Playboy,* January 1964, p. 213)

4. Develop some paragraphs by an extended example:

> The most elementary example of the unforeseeable effects of technical progress is furnished by drugs. You have a cold in the head; you take an aspirin. The headache disappears, but aspirin has other actions besides doing away with headaches. In the beginning we were really oblivious of these side effects; but, I should imagine, by now everyone has read articles warning against the use of aspirin because of its possible effects, say, on the blood picture. Grave hemorrhages have appeared in people who habitually took two or three aspirins daily. Yet aspirin was thought the perfect remedy a scant ten years ago—on the ground that no side effects were to be feared. Now such effects begin to appear in what was, and is, probably the most harmless of all drugs.
>
> —Jacques Ellul, "Technological Progress Is Always Ambiguous" (John Wilkinson, trans., *Technology and Culture,* Fall 1962)

5. Develop some paragraphs by an anecdote—that is, by a story told to illustrate your point:

> . . . But miracles *do* happen in Monte Carlo. Years ago at the elegant Summer Sporting Club, where roulette tables are on the terrace, the croupier said, "Rien ne va plus," when a 100-franc chip dropped down from heaven and fell into the slot of number eight. A second later the ball fell into the slot of number eight. A lady on the balcony who had lost all her money had found another chip in her purse, got mad and threw it over the balustrade. She won 3500 francs, came down to collect, stayed at the table and lost everything. That's a true story, and a sad one.
>
> —Joseph Wechsberg, "The Lore and Lure of Roulette" (*Playboy,* January 1967, p. 116)

6. Develop some paragraphs by hypothetical illustration—that is, by examples or stories invented to illustrate your ideas:

An egghead is anyone who seems to be so absorbed in the pursuit of knowledge that he hardly sees the obvious pleasures of life— "partying" three times a week, "getting wasted" on Saturday night, and lying to your parents about your reasons for staggering home at three in the morning when curfew is at twelve sharp. Instead of living, the egghead thinks. For example, consider Jonathan Square. Does he ever date girls, go to dances, watch television, or listen to "together" music? The answer is definitely "No!" When I see him in the hall each morning, his head is bent, his feet shuffle lethargically, his back twists into a question mark above the twelve books under his right arm; his appearance unequivocally suggests lofty contemplation. At noon, while everyone else gossips and giggles, Jon Square sits silently in a corner, thumbing the worn pages of a massive philosophy text; from time to time, his eyes glaze over like a lizard's. And what he does in the evening is no secret to anyone; while Mozart tinkles away, or Beethoven blares, Jonathan Square nods and dreams over his books or reflects on the human condition and the sadness of the world without joy.

7. Develop some paragraphs by analogy—that is, by an extended point-by-point comparison:

They made a robot in the shape of a dragonfly and named it Ranger VII, thereby expressing their hope that it would range the face of the moon. For eyes, they gave it camera lenses, and taught it how to photograph by blinking the shutters. Near the place where its nose should have been, they

put a radio antenna like a saucer, and taught
the robot how to send pictures back through
the saucer to earth. When all this was done,
they folded the dragonfly's wings, set the
mechanical insect on top of a rocket, and fired
the rocket into orbit around the earth. Finally
they shot the robot out of the orbit, told it to
unfold its wings, and pointed it onto a curving
path across 243,665 miles of sky. The path
ended in a dry lunar lakebed that hadn't been
thought important enough to be named.

—John Lear, "What the Moon Ranger Couldn't
See" (*Saturday Review,* September 5, 1964, p. 35)

8. Develop some paragraphs by definition:

What, therefore, is a cliché? Perhaps
intellectual and intelligent opinion has not yet
been so far crystallized as to justify a
definition. The *Oxford English Dictionary* says
that it is "a stereotyped expression, a
commonplace phrase." I should . . . like to
enlarge on that definition and render it more
practical, more comprehensive. The origin of
the term may help, for as Littré shows, *cliché*
is the substantivized participle of *clicher,* a
variant of *cliquer,* "to *click*"; *clicher* is a die
sinker's term for "to strike melted lead in
order to obtain a cast"; hence, a cliché is a
stereotyped expression—a phrase "on tap" as it
were—and this derivative sense, which has
been current in France since the early eighties,
came to England *ca.* 1890. *Revenons à nos
moutons* (cliché). A *cliché* is an outworn
commonplace; a phrase, or short sentence, that
has become so hackneyed that careful
speakers and scrupulous writers shrink from it
because they feel that its use is an insult to
the intelligence of their audience or public: "a
coin so battered by use as to be defaced"
(George Baker). Clichés range from flyblown

phrases ("much of a muchness"; "to all intents and purposes"), metaphors that are now pointless ("lock, stock and barrel"), formulas that have become mere counters ("far be it from me to . . .")—through sobriquets that have lost all their freshness and most of their significance ("the Iron Duke")—to quotations that are nauseating ("cups that cheer but not inebriate"), and foreign phrases that are tags *("longo intervallo," "bête noire")*.

—Eric Partridge, *Dictionary of Clichés*
(New York: Macmillan, 1950)

9. Develop some paragraphs by an appeal to authority—that is, by quoting and paraphrasing a reliable source:

Actually, however, most primitive peoples believe that the head and all its hairs are occupied by spirits, and are taboo to the touch. In *The Golden Bough,* Sir James George Frazer's masterwork on myths, folklore and religion, the anthropologist records that if a Maori so much as scratched his head with his fingers, "he was immediately obliged to apply them to his nose, and snuff up the sanctity which they had acquired by the touch," and the son of a Marquesan high priest "has been seen to roll on the ground in an agony of rage and despair, begging for death, because someone had desecrated his head and deprived him of his divinity by sprinkling a few drops of water on his hair."

—William Iverson, "A Short History of Shaves and Haircuts" (*Playboy*, November 1964, p. 117)

10. Develop some paragraphs by a combination of methods:

Today no one bestrides our narrow world like a colossus; we have no giants who play roles which one can imagine no one else playing in their stead. There are a few figures on the margin of uniqueness, perhaps: Adenauer, Nehru, Tito, De Gaulle, Chiang Kai-shek, Mao Tse-tung. But there seems to be none in the epic style of those mighty figures of our recent past who seized history with both hands and gave it an imprint, even a direction, which it otherwise might not have had. As De Gaulle himself remarked on hearing of Stalin's death, "The age of giants is over." Whatever one thought, whether one admired or detested Roosevelt or Churchill, Stalin or Hitler, one nevertheless felt the sheer weight of such personalities on one's own existence. We feel no comparable pressures today. Our own President, with all his pleasant qualities, has more or less explicitly renounced any desire to impress his own views on history. The Macmillans, Khrushchevs and Gronchis have measurably less specific gravity than their predecessors. Other men could be in their places as leaders of America or Britain or Russia or Italy without any change in the course of history. Why ours should thus be an age without heroes, and whether this condition is good or bad for us and for civilization, are topics worthy of investigation.

—Arthur M. Schlesinger, Jr.,
"The Decline of Greatness"
(*The Saturday Evening Post*,
November 1, 1958, p. 25)

dia

Dialogue: Problems in Punctuation—In writing dialogue, observe the conventions of punctuation and paragraphing.

1. Use a comma with the verb of saying:

"I'm just fine," Bradford said.

Bradford said, "I'm just fine."

2. Use a question mark or exclamation point if the dialogue requires it:

"How are you?" Bradford asked.

Bradford asked, "How are you?"

"Hey!" Bradford said.

Bradford said, "Hey!"

3. When the verb of saying interrupts a complete sentence, set off the verb with commas:

"You know," Bradford said, "I've had that camera for years and never used it."

4. When the verb of saying ends a complete sentence and is followed by a new sentence spoken by the same person, (a) place a period after the verb and (b) begin the new sentence with a quotation mark and a capital letter:

"I want to write a song for you," Bradford said. "What's your name?"

5. Since written dialogue represents the speech of two or more persons, conventions require that you begin a new paragraph with each new speaker, no matter how short his or her bit of dialogue. Brief passages of description and narrative are usually included as part of the new paragraph:

"My name is Karen."

"Do you like hard rock?" he asked.

She said, "Of course."

"I have just the thing for you, then," he said. "I can write a song called 'Your Eyes Are Mine.' Would you like that?"

"I'd like that very much," Karen replied, shaking her hair back out of her eyes. "Do you write songs for every girl you meet?"

Bradford smiled. "No," he said, "I sometimes write poems."

His friend James Barton interrupted, looking up over his cup of coffee. "You sometimes go so far so fast there's no time for poetry or songs."

"There's always time for poetry."

"Yeh?"

Bradford said, a smile twitching under his moustache, "For sure, buddy—and you know it."

(See **Quotation Marks.**)

---

div

Division (of words into syllables)—When the last word of a line must be continued on the next line, divide the word only between syllables.

As a general rule, divide as seldom as possible, and never divide the last word on a page. Always check the syllabification of a word in your dictionary: you *cannot* rely on guesswork or reasoning.

ORIGINAL

The image James Dean presented
in his movie rol-
es was that of a petul-
ant boy, skirting the
brink of delinquency.
(*Roles* cannot be divided because
it has only one syllable. *Petulant*
is properly divided in this way:
pet-u-lant.)

REVISION

The image James Dean
presented in his movie roles
was that of a petu-
lant boy, skirting
the brink of delinquency.
(*Roles* is not divided. *Petulant* is divided properly between syllables.)

---

e . . .   **Ellipsis**—Use ellipsis marks (three periods) to show omissions from quoted material.

ORIGINAL

"He sat down and deliberated until he developed an explanation for the events of the last weeks."

"Classification is closely related to analysis; in fact, it is sometimes seen as an aspect of the same mental process. But there is a difference."

ELLIPTICAL TEXT

"He . . . developed an explanation for the events of the last weeks." (Ellipsis marks used in place of omitted material.)

"Classification is closely related to analysis. . . . But there is a difference." (Note that when the ellipsis comes at the end of a sentence, you must also add a period, making a total of *four* "periods.")

Use a full line of spaced periods to indicate omission of an entire paragraph or one or more entire lines of poetry.

ORIGINAL

Whenas in silks my Julia goes,
Then, then, methinks how sweetly
  flows

ELLIPTICAL TEXT

Whenas in silks my Julia goes,
Then, then, methinks how sweetly
  flows

The liquefaction of her clothes.
Next, when I cast mine eyes and
   see
That brave vibration each way
   free,
Oh, how that glittering taketh me!

> —Robert Herrick,
> "Upon Julia's Clothes"

The liquefaction of her clothes.
....
Oh, how that glittering taketh me!

Exclamation Point—Use the exclamation point (!) after an emphatic word, phrase, or clause.

Word

"Stop!"
"Damn!"

Phrase

"What a beautiful car!"

Clause

"He *can't* be guilty!"

Place the exclamation point inside quotation marks when it is part of the quoted material; otherwise, place it outside:

The usher shouted, "Clear the aisles!"

Look at those "creeps"!

Do not use a period or a comma with an exclamation point:

ORIGINAL

"Get away from there!," he shouted.

REVISION

"Get away from there!" he shouted.

In standard expository prose, do not use more than one exclamation point at a time:

ORIGINAL

"Stay away from my daughter!!!!"
Daddy said to my boyfriend.

REVISION

"Stay away from my daughter!"
Daddy said to my boyfriend.

Do not use an exclamation mark for a mild command:

ORIGINAL

Try not to be late for dinner, dear!

REVISION

Try not to be late for dinner, dear.

f

frag

Fragmentary Sentence—Do not write grammatically incomplete sentences.

To do so, in the minds of many English teachers, is a crime against common sense and good manners, especially in writing rather formal expository prose, where the writer is required to demonstrate his command of grammar, style, and sentence structure in *every* sentence. A bit of an overreaction, perhaps. Almost everyone writes sentence fragments from time to time—like the sentence just before this one. Many professional writers use sentence fragments freely and effectively; some novelists have built whole careers on them. But there's a difference. What knowledgeable writers do instinctively and well, student writers often do ineffectively, out of ignorance and inexperience. Our advice, then, is to avoid sentence fragments altogether, especially in expository writing, unless you can justify each of them in a footnote.

The following *types* of sentence fragments occur frequently:

1. Subordinate clauses punctuated as complete sentences:

Subordinate clauses are clauses introduced by subordinate conjunctions—words such as *if, because, since, when, although, though,* and *whereas.* Even though such a clause has, by definition, both a subject and a verb, it does not express a complete thought and should not be punctuated as a complete sentence.

ORIGINAL

John cannot come to the party. *Because he is ill.*

Meanwhile our government is paying farmers not to grow crops. *While all over the world people are living out of garbage cans.*

REVISION

John cannot come to the party *because* he is ill.

Meanwhile our government is paying farmers not to grow crops, *while all over the world people are living out of garbage cans.*

2. Verbal phrases punctuated as complete sentences:

ORIGINAL

Tom, *working hard on his book.* (This verbal phrase cannot stand alone as a sentence. Either the phrase must be changed to a clause or something else must be added to make the sentence complete.)

Even as it is, newspapers no longer seem very profitable. *Witnessed by the fact that in many large cities, the dailies have had to consolidate to survive as one instead of dying as two or more.*

REVISION

Tom, *working hard on his book, failed to remember his wedding anniversary.*

OR:

Tom *was working hard on his book.*

Even as it is, newspapers no longer seem very profitable, *witnessed by the fact that in many large cities, the dailies have had to consolidate to survive as one instead of dying as two or more.*

Each week many violent shows blaze across the TV screen. *Adding color and variety to the dull lives of the masses.*

Each week many violent shows blaze across the TV screen, *adding color and variety to the dull lives of the masses.* (The error is corrected in these last two examples by joining the sentence fragment to the preceding sentence, where it properly belongs. But both fragments seemed to occur because the writers wanted to *emphasize* the idea contained in the phrase. Hence, although their grammar was incorrect, their motives were pure.)

3. Appositives (nouns or noun substitutes) punctuated as complete sentences:

ORIGINAL

Nowhere in the civilized world is man totally free of social pressure. *A pressure he has created himself.* (The appositive, improperly punctuated as a complete sentence, is grammatically a part of the preceding sentence.)

Man, in his never-ending race with success, has created an economic system which has only served to further enslave him in the materialistic life. *A life based on greed, guilt, exploitation and hate.* (This very emphatic statement *should* be set off—by a dash.)

REVISION

Nowhere in the civilized world is man totally free of social pressure—*a pressure he has created himself.* (The dash emphasizes the idea contained in the fragment and makes the fragment part of the preceding sentence.)

Man, in his never-ending race with success, has created an economic system which has only served to further enslave him in the materialistic life—*a life based on greed, guilt, exploitation and hate.* (Now the appositive is an emphatic part of the preceding sentence.)

4. Part of a compound predicate punctuated as a complete sentence when it should be an integral part of the preceding sentence:

ORIGINAL

Sam is an excellent optometrist. *And has a lucrative practice as a result.*

REVISION

Sam is an excellent optometrist *and has a lucrative practice as a result.*

The man from the telephone company installed my phone. *And then stayed for a martini.* (In both examples, the second sentence is simply part of a compound predicate that belongs, grammatically, to the preceding sentence.)

The man from the telephone company installed my phone *and then stayed for a martini.*

h

Hyphen—Hyphenate the last word in a line where necessary; hyphenate certain compound words; use hyphens for clarity.

1. Hyphenate the last word in a line where necessary (see **Division**):

> From their report, he sensed that the members of the entertainment committee were ignorant of the club's actual fiscal condition.

Note: Divide words only at syllables. Do not divide a word without first checking its syllabification in your dictionary.

2. Hyphenate certain compound words:
(a) Use a hyphen after the suffix *-elect*:

> president-elect

(b) Use a hyphen after the prefixes *ex-*, *self-*, and *all-*:

> ex-wife
>
> self-inflicted
>
> all-inclusive

(c) Use a hyphen after a prefix that precedes a proper noun:

pro-administration

anti-government

pre-World War II

(d) Use a hyphen after a prefix ending in *i*- or *a*- when the root word begins with the same letter:

semi-independent

extra-atmospheric

(e) Hyphenate compound adjectives which immediately precede a noun:

He gained a hard-won victory.

She resembled a two-ton truck.

I left on a well-earned vacation.

This is take-a-good-friend-to-lunch week.

Note: Compound adjectives that occur after the noun generally are not hyphenated:

His attitude was clearly one of *devil may care.*

My vacation was *well earned.*

His victory was *hard won.*

(f) Hyphenate numbers 21 to 99 wherever they occur:

I am thirty-three now, but I'll be thirty-four soon.

There are forty-five girls in the topless show at Big Al's.

(g) Hyphenate certain compound nouns:

mother-in-law; has-been; man-made

Since rules governing the use of hyphens with compound nouns vary with time and usage, you should consult your dictionary when writing virtually any of them.

3. Hyphenate for clarity:

To get her mind off that horrible day, she sought a new form of *recreation*.

As part of the centennial celebration, the town's citizens attempted a *re-creation* of the famous Battle of Groaning Board that took place there in 1876.

He wore his light blue suit. (The suit is light in weight and blue in color.)

He wore his light-blue suit. (The suit's color is a light blue.)

i

imp

Impersonal Construction—Avoid impersonal constructions wherever possible.

Impersonal constructions are not *bad:* they are weak; they lack force; they soften your prose. These consequences result from the nature of the impersonal construction: it is a subject-verb combination in which the subject refers to nothing definite and the verb expresses little or no *action*. For example, *"It was believed* that the student rebellion was a communist plot." The pronoun *it* has no antecedent; *believed* expresses a state of mind. *"There are* hordes of people milling around the accident." In this sentence, the expletive *there* displaces the subject *(hordes)* and forces a flabby verb *(are)* into the sentence. Far better to say: "I believe the student rebellion was a communist plot." Or: "Hordes of people mill around the accident."

Note, however, that the very nature of the language requires *some* impersonal constructions: *"It seems* cold in here." "It is snowing."

Nevertheless, you should try to change every impersonal construction to more forceful, more direct constructions, as in the following examples:

ORIGINAL	REVISION
It was very crowded: *there were* a lot of people at the party.	A lot of people came to the party: people sat in every chair, stood and chatted in the middle of the room, and reclined in corners, sucking in the evil fumes of Indian hemp.
It seemed to me that every time I turned around, *there was* somebody asking for another drink.	I rushed about all evening, jumping up every time I sat down, as my guests kept asking for more drinks.

intro **Introduction**—The first paragraph of an essay should try to do two things: (1) interest the reader; (2) state the thesis.

The basic technique is simple: don't begin by taking two steps backward; instead, dive into your subject. In doing so, you can catch the attention of your reader in many ways, a few of which we will comment on here. When you have him "hooked," give him your thesis immediately—at the end of the first paragraph, if possible.

Narrative Introductions

The narrative introduction begins with a brief story; it shows people *acting,* as in this opening paragraph from an essay on college students during the Great Depression of the 1930s. The thesis is stated at the beginning of the second paragraph:

> Across the campus of Oklahoma A. and M. College moved a weird procession. At the front was an ancient open flivver sufficiently

battered to be termed "collegiate." In its front
seat were two boys; in its back seat a bale of
hay. There followed another car, differing
from the first only in the number and kind of
dents in its fenders and body. It was also
manned by two boys. Its back seat was
occupied by a large crate of protesting poultry.
Then came a fifth boy leading a Jersey cow.
The cow refused to be influenced by the obvious impatience of the motorized portion of the
procession, so it was hours later when the
strange group finally arrived in front of a house
on the outskirts of the college town. The
poultry was given a back yard coop in which
to live and, presumably, to lay eggs. The cow
was tethered in an adjoining field. Then from
some recesses in the battered hulls of the
flivvers the boys pulled out some 200 quarts of
canned fruits and vegetables and a dozen
cured hams. With meat and vegetables in the
cellar and prospective eggs and milk in the
back yard, the five were ready for higher education.

*College students have probably developed
more ingenious ways of beating the depression than any other group in America.*

—Gilbert Love, "College Students Are
Beating the Depression" *(School and
Society,* XXXVIII, June 10, 1933)

Or look at this narrative opening: it uses a brief,
humorous incident to set the stage for the thesis
statement at the end of the second paragraph.
(Actually, the concept is one paragraph; the
paragraph division occurs because of the dialogue.)

On vacation in rural New England, the
president of an Eastern university woke up
one night with sharp abdominal pains. He got

to the nearest hospital, where a local technician took a sample of his blood and confirmed the doctor's verdict: appendicitis. Everything was being readied for the operation, when the surgeon learned that his patient, like himself, was a Rotarian. At this news he paused.

"Better do that blood test again," he said thoughtfully. "The lab girl isn't very good." A fresh sample was taken, and this time the white count proved normal. His appendix in fine shape—he had nothing more than indigestion—the educator left the hospital with his faith in Rotarians unshaken. *But he vowed never again to place blind trust in a medical laboratory.*

—Maya Pines, "Danger in Our Medical Labs"
(Harper's Magazine, October 1963, p. 84)

Expository Introductions

The expository opening begins by explaining or describing. Sometimes the expository opening paragraph is little more than a thesis statement. In that case, the writer often tries to capture his reader's interest with a startling thesis statement or a bit of catchy phrasing, as in this paragraph from Welles Hangen's "Stirrings Behind the Wall: East Germany's Muted Revolution":

Robert Havemann, the scientist, could never be compared to Galileo, but Robert Havemann the heretic is more remarkable. *He has refused to recant.*

—*Harper's Magazine,* May 1965

And sometimes it is a carefully detailed description:

Look at him. A tall, lanky, young man, aged thirty, with a ready boyish smile and charm

that is almost a tool. Blue-gray eyes, a
handsome face, a sensitive mouth, blond hair.
He likes flashy clothes, Italian shoes, tight
trousers, colorful sweaters. Does he really
come from Moscow, or from Saint Germain
des Pres, Via Veneto, or Greenwich Village?
Why is he the idol of Soviet youth, who recite
his poems by heart? Why do the Russians first
promote him at home, send him abroad on
almost official assignments—and then suddenly
unleash the whole Soviet propaganda
apparatus in an attempt to destroy him? Is he
a showman or poet, prophet or opportunist,
rebel or Soviet propagandist-at-large? *Who are
you, Evgeny Evtushenko?*

> —Michael Gordey, "Consider Me a
> Communist" (*Harper's Magazine,*
> October 1963)

Another way to get the interest of your reader
in an expository introduction is to begin with a
direct quotation—sometimes from a literary
source, sometimes from a central figure expressing
an important idea or attitude in your essay. Look
at the next paragraph, for example: a direct
quotation introduces the subject and at the same
time leads to the thesis statement in the last
sentence in the paragraph.

"It's not my fault! Nothing in this lousy world
is my fault, don't you see that? I don't want it
to be and it can't be and it won't be." This
outcry comes from Kerouac's Sal Paradise, but
it expresses the deep conviction of multitudes
of irresponsibles in the age of self-pity. *It is a
curious paradox that, while the self is the
center of all things, the self is never to blame
for anything.*

> —Robert Elliot Fitch, "The Irresponsibles,"
> *Odyssey of the Self-Centered Self* (New York:
> Harcourt Brace Jovanovich, 1960, 1961)

Finally, we come to the type of expository opening paragraph that gets interest by presenting facts and figures of a rather startling nature, as in this opening paragraph:

> Over one million Americans have already been slaughtered in highway accidents. A million more will be killed over the next 15 years. *Irate safety experts say that fully two-thirds of all traffic victims could be spared their lives if auto manufacturers could place less emphasis on "styling" and more on "crash-worthiness."*
>
> —Ralph Ginzburg, "S.O.B. Detroit"
> (*Fact,* May–June 1964)

In brief, the good introduction, like a short skirt or a flashy car, gets attention: it says, "Look!" But it does more than that, of course—for it also leads to the thesis statement, often the last sentence of the first paragraph or the first sentence of the second paragraph; and on your thesis statement hangs all the rest of the essay.

ital

Italics—Use italics (underlining, in handwritten and typed manuscripts) for certain titles, words and expressions, letters, numbers, and names.

1. Use italics for the titles of newspapers, magazines, pamphlets, books, paintings, sculptures, plays, films, television shows, and musical productions:

NEWSPAPERS

the San Francisco *Examiner* (or the *San Francisco Examiner*)

the New York *Times* (or the *New York Times*)

MAGAZINES

National Geographic

Redbook

PAMPHLETS

Tom Paine's *Common Sense*

BOOKS

The Grapes of Wrath

Rhetoric in a Modern Mode

PAINTINGS AND SCULPTURE

Titian's *Sacred and Profane Love*

Rembrandt's *The Night Watch*

Michelangelo's *David*

PLAYS

Edward Albee's *Who's Afraid of Virginia Woolf?*

Shakespeare's *Romeo and Juliet*

FILMS

Harold Lloyd's *The Freshman*

The Godfather

TELEVISION SHOWS

All in the Family

Sesame Street

MUSICAL PRODUCTIONS

Oklahoma!

Funny Girl

Verdi's *Il Trovatore*

Note: *Use quotation marks, not italics, for the titles of unpublished manuscripts, book chapters, short stories, reviews, articles, songs, and brief poems. (See* **Quotation Marks.***)*

2. Use italics for words, letters, numbers, and symbols used as such:

WORDS

His sentences suffer from too many *and's*.

LETTERS

The *e* in *come* is silent.

Students frequently leave out the *o* in *environment*.

NUMBERS

Her *3's* and *8's* look very much alike.

SYMBOLS

To get the area of a circle, use the formula πr^2.

Avoid the use of *&* in place of *and*.

3. Use italics for foreign words or expressions not yet anglicized:

deo volente

bête noire

cherchez la femme

sic

4. Use italics to emphasize certain words and expressions:

"What do you *mean?*" I demanded.

"Guess what? I have a date with *her!*"

5. Use italics for the names of ships, trains, and airplanes:

The P & O Liner *Orsova* has a reputation for fine food and service.

Southern Pacific's once famous *City of San Francisco* is now history.

Miraculously no one was injured when Japan Air Line's DC-8 *Shiga* accidentally landed in San Francisco Bay.

1

Logic—In writing anything, use clear, careful logic and sound common sense.

If a passage is marked *Logic?* in one of your essays, your instructor means that what you have written is not reasoned: it lacks real thought, convincing evidence of good judgment, rationally persuasive deductions. The question *logic?* really means *"Think!"*

You should, however, be able to recognize certain logical fallacies that you might conceivably commit and will certainly come across in your everyday reading of magazines, newspapers, letters, even textbooks. Such fallacies crop up with even greater frequency—and greater immunity—in conversation, all the more reason to know them by name. Hence you should learn to recognize and analyze the following common logical fallacies: *abstractions; appeal to emotions; causation; false analogy; hasty generalization; name-calling; non sequiturs; undefined terms;* and *unqualified generalizations.*

1. Abstractions:

Abstract words describe qualities common to a *group* of things—*beauty, toughness, difficulty.* They also name spiritual, intellectual, and emotional states—*honesty, immorality, fear.* Such words are absolutely necessary to all thought and writing, certainly; but be wary. Some abstract words are like bear traps. Concealed by the tangle of language, they lie hidden, ready to grab and cripple you. *Communism, Americanism, welfare state, racism, pacifism*—when you get carelessly close to these words, your writing is in real danger, because you are walking in a field laden with emotional snares. *The American way of life,* you feel, is an extraordinarily good thing; we agree. But *don't* write about it as though it were real, like a car, which you can get into, drive away, and park under a full moon. *It is an abstraction.* Treat it as such. Acknowledge that millions of Americans share it—but millions of others don't. And how much of it and what each group shares differs from individual to individual, and the differences change almost hourly. Thus you must not write, "The American way of life is threatened by the international communist conspiracy, which hopes to exploit the growing racism of our welfare state in order to destroy Americanism completely." *Logic?* What do those words *mean?* Where did you get these ideas? How can you prove them? In other words, you're being excessively emotional, and your emotions have whirled you into a logical vacuum where *words* have become *things.* Beware the abstraction.

2. Appeal to Emotions:

In expository and argumentative writing, it is unfair to appeal strongly to your reader's emotions: you sway his judgment by twisting his feelings. Thus, in arguing about capital punishment, you should avoid the temptation to tell your reader in gruesome detail exactly how the condemned man suffers, or how, because of his childhood, he couldn't help himself. *His father, an alcoholic, beat him without mercy; his mother, a full-time slut and a part-time prostitute, let him go hungry all day long, his diapers unchanged for days, when he was only two years old. Does this man deserve to die, even though he tortured four people to death?*

Maybe not, but that's no argument against capital punishment: it's an attempt to make us feel sorry for a particular murderer and thereby make us condemn a legal procedure. It is good rhetorical strategy, perhaps, but a critical reader will spot it—and condemn it—for what it is: a logically unjustified appeal to our emotions.

3. Causation:

The fallacy of causation is known in logic as the *post hoc, ergo propter hoc* fallacy. The Latin means, "After this, therefore because of this." That is, it designates the fallacious belief that one event *necessarily* causes another that follows it. "Tom's grades dropped after he bought that motorcycle. I knew that cycle would interfere with his studies." Good reasoning? No—something else might have caused Tom's grades to drop, like a serious case of depression. More likely, however, a *combination* of causes brought about this particular result. Perhaps Tom got his motorcycle just before he broke up with his girl; perhaps, besides that, his parents are troubled, and Tom may be sensitive to their condition; perhaps, moreover, Tom has a new teacher who is particularly demanding. *Any* number of causes might account for the change in Tom's grades. It is probably true, in fact, that for every result there is a complicated set of causes. Certainly it is *not* true that anything which immediately follows an event has been *caused* by that event. Beware the fallacy of causation.

4. False Analogy:

Analogy is an extended, point-by-point
comparison of two essentially dissimilar things. It
follows therefore that an analogy can be used
only to illustrate a point, never to prove it. In this
sense, then, analogies used in argumentation are
always false, because they misleadingly seem to
offer the substance of logical reasoning. For
example, let's argue that men are not free to
choose their own destiny, that every event in life
is determined for every individual. We might
argue by this analogy: "Life is like a great chess
game. God, or some other force just as powerful,
is playing a kind of game with Himself, using us
as pawns, while a special few are knights and
bishops, or kings and queens. He moves you one
square as he attacks, say, the white queen by
putting pressure on one of her bishops. Then he
deliberately sacrifices you in order to improve his
position. Boooom! You're dead, man, knocked off
by the queen's bishop. And what does it all
mean? Nothing. It's just a game, an absurd game,
and your life is just as absurd and meaningless as
mine, or Queen Elizabeth's. Life is a farce."

Now that is an interesting analogy—sophomoric,
but interesting. What does it prove? As the man
said, "Nothing. It's just a game. . . ." Anybody can
make any kind of analogy he pleases; he still
proves nothing, no matter how convincing he
sounds. All analogies, therefore, must be used
with care—because all analogies are false
analogies.

5. Hasty Generalization:

A hasty generalization is a general statement
based on too few instances. "My adopted daughter
Lisa is very bright and very beautiful. My adopted
son Jonathan is a bright and beautiful boy. All
adopted children must be bright and beautiful."
Not true: some adopted children, like some
teachers, must be plain and dull; some adopted

children, like some college students, must have
average looks and average minds. In fact, as we
all know, we can expect infinite variations in
adopted children—even in Jonathan and Lisa, who
are probably alike in very few ways.

Do not try to prove a broad general statement
with only a few instances. (See also *Unqualified
Generalizations,* p. 82.)

6. Name-calling:

Name-calling is a logical fallacy only when you
fail to show that the unfavorable expressions you
have applied to the subject under discussion are
accurate, valid descriptions. "I am a decent,
civilized man. But John, who opposes me, is an
arrogant son-of-a-bitch." That's name-calling—an
unfair tactic in argument or debate. On the other
hand, if you can substantiate your accusations,
you are on sounder logical ground. First of all,
define your terms. What is an *arrogant son-of-a-
bitch?* Secondly, show that John really does
have the qualities set forth in your definition.
Then, depending on how sound your definition
is, you may have a valid criticism of John instead
of an emotional, unreasoning condemnation.

7. Non Sequiturs:

Non sequitur, in Latin, means, "It does not follow." Let us use the term in a very broad sense to
designate a conclusion that does not follow logically from the evidence on which it is based—
usually not evidence at all, in fact, but a universal
generalization accepted without question. "He
must be awfully lazy if he's on welfare." This is
a non sequitur because the statement includes the
questionable assumption that only *lazy* men and
women are on welfare. If you think at all, however, you'll soon realize that this assumption is
not fair or valid because many people on welfare
are simply unfortunate victims of circumstances:
children on welfare, for instance, or men whose

crafts have been hit by an economic recession, such as happens periodically in aerospace industries.

Other non sequiturs may be analyzed in the same way: "Well, he's from Alabama—obviously he's a segregationist." "He's not a communist; after all, he attends Mass regularly." "He's Black, so he can really sing and dance." It does not follow that a man from Alabama is necessarily a segregationist. It does not follow that someone who attends Mass regularly is, say, a Democrat instead of a communist. And it does not follow that all Blacks sing and dance well. Each of these non sequiturs is based on an unquestioned, highly general assumption rather than on logical evidence.

8. Undefined Terms:

Often an argument is simply meaningless because the writer has failed to define his terms accurately or at all. Has the war in Vietnam been an act of genocide, for instance? Without a full definition of the word *genocide,* we can circle this question as energetically as a dog chases its own tail—with about as much result. Now, *genocide* cooperates: it is an easy word to define. It means, according to *Webster's Third New International Dictionary of the English Language* (Springfield, Massachusetts: G. & C. Merriam Company, Publishers, 1961), "the use of deliberate systematic measures (as killing, bodily or mental injury, unlivable conditions, preventions of births) calculated to bring about the extermination of a racial, political, or cultural group or to destroy the language, religion, or culture of a group." With *evidence* of genocide, one may take the argument from there: at least there would be some point in proceeding.

But other words are much more difficult to pin down. *Americanism? Communism?* Do they seem too hard to define? Well, then, take an easy word, like *nice.* We all know what *nice* means, don't we? It has at least fifteen *basic* meanings, according to the *Oxford English Dictionary*. Its early meanings—"foolish, stupid, senseless"; "wanton, loose-mannered, lascivious"—are not so nice at all.

Is she a nice girl—or isn't she? Not even *she* knows for sure.

Nothing can be gained in argumentation without full and accurate definition of important terms.

9. Unqualified Generalizations:

A generalization is a broad statement about a number of particulars; a concept or an idea about a group of things drawn from observation of them. Unfortunately, most of the generalizations that sail blithely through our speech and writing are not our own ideas but someone else's, absorbed like oxygen from the atmosphere. The Japanese, for example, believe that Koreans are cruel and Chinese are dirty, stupid, and untrustworthy. The Koreans, on the other hand, hold similar beliefs about the Japanese and Chinese, and the Chinese think of Koreans and Japanese in much the same way.

What we have just said may be partly true. But if you accepted these general statements as *the* truth, then we have hoodwinked you—with a set of *unqualified* generalizations. Some Japanese may be prejudiced against Koreans; *some* Koreans may hate the Chinese; *a few* Chinese may loathe all Koreans, Japanese, Russians, Germans, Blacks, and Jews. But not *all*, certainly, in any of these cases. Hence the generalizations must be *qualified*.

In making general statements, then, use words like *some, many, most, a few, perhaps, maybe, possibly*, and conditional verbs like *may* and *might*. Even so, "we may be tempted to agree with Justice Holmes that 'the chief end of man is to frame general propositions, and no general proposition is worth a damn" (Lionel Ruby, "Are All Generalizations False?" from *The Art of Making Sense*, Philadelphia: Lippincott, 1954).

lc

Lower-Case Letters—Do not use unnecessary capital letters. Use lower-case letters instead, especially for common nouns, points of the compass, and certain other common constructions. (See **Capitalization.**)

1. Common nouns:

He is a junior in college.

He plans to major in history.

Wisconsin in the fall is an explosion of color.

2. Points of the compass:

He is heading east for his vacation.

The aircraft headed north, then east, and finally settled on a northeasterly course.

3. Family relationships when used with possessive pronouns:

Mr. and Mrs. Smith will visit his mother.

(BUT: We will visit Mother today.)

Because he needed money, John wrote a long letter to his father.

(BUT: John wrote to Father asking for more money.)

4. After a semicolon:

Simon will go to Chicago; he plans to visit with his grandfather.

The books are by the same author; however, the quality of the writing is extremely uneven.

5. For the first word after an interrupted quotation:

"We can't go," he said, "because tonight we have to study our math."

"I will attend the University of Oslo this summer," he said, "in order to learn the Norwegian language."

6. For the first word in a quotation that is not a complete sentence:

He wrote that Wednesday's meeting would be "one of the most crucial" in the history of the student body.

This piece of legislation, according to our representatives, "must be defeated."

---

ms

Manuscript Preparation—Prepare your manuscript exactly as directed by your instructor, or follow these generally accepted standards established by the Modern Language Association:

1. Either type your manuscript or use a pen with blue or black ink.

2. *Paper.* Type on one side only of good white paper, 8½ by 11 inches in size. If you do not type, use standard composition paper (notebook paper)—*not paper torn from a spiral binder.*

3. *Typing.* Type with double-spacing throughout, except for long quotations, which should be single-spaced and set off from the body of the manuscript by wider margins. *If you use a pen, skip every other line.*

4. *Margins.* Consistently leave margins of from 1 to 1½ inches at the top, bottom, and sides of each page *except the first.* The first page is special. On

the first page, center the title of your essay about two inches from the top of the page; then start your first line about 1 inch below the title.

5. *Title page.* Your title page is a cover for your essay. Center your title halfway down the page. In the top right hand corner, endorse your paper with the following information: your name; the course; the date on which the paper is handed in.

Example: Richard Savage
                Communications 11, MFW 2
                January 1, 1984

6. *Pagination.* Beginning with page 2, number your pages consecutively throughout the manuscript, placing the number in the right-hand corner at the top of the page.

Note: Your title page, being only a cover, is not counted as part of your manuscript and, of course, is not numbered. Since your first page—which has the title of your essay at the top of the page —is *obviously* your first page, it does not need to have the number 1 written on it. (See **Titles**.)

mar   **Margins**—Leave generous margins—from 1 to 1½ inches—at the top, bottom, and both sides of your paper.

Although a page with generous margins is more attractive than a cramped, crowded page, this rule has little to do with the appearance of your paper; it is designed, instead, to give your instructor sufficient space for comments, questions, and corrections.

While no one expects an even right-hand margin, you can avoid a ragged margin by the judicious use of hyphens. (See **Hyphens** and **Division**.)

mm   **Misplaced Modifiers**—To say clearly and precisely what you mean, place modifiers as close to the modified words as possible.

A modifier is a word, phrase, or clause that qualifies, limits, or restricts the meaning of another word or phrase. In order to prevent confusion, modifiers must be clearly related to what they modify. When the relationship is not clear, the modifier is misplaced—that is, in the wrong part of the sentence.

ORIGINAL

John sold the car to a friend *that had a bent fender.* (The friend had a bent fender?)

The man chased the chicken with a butcher knife, which was so scared it ran right at him. (The butcher knife was scared?)

REVISION

John sold the car *that had a bent fender* to a friend. (The modifier is now properly placed.)

With a butcher knife, the man chased the chicken, which was so scared it ran right at him.

Note how the writer changes the meaning of each sentence below by shifting the modifier *only:*

He *only* asked me for my book.

Only he asked me for my book.

He asked me *only* for my book.

He asked me for my book *only.*

He asked me for my *only* book.

num

Numbers—Use Arabic numerals for numbers in dates; addresses; telephone numbers; hours and minutes written as A.M. or P.M.; decimals; certain travel information; certain data about books; and all other numbers that cannot be written in one or two words. For most other uses, spell out the number instead of writing it in Arabic numerals.

1. Dates:

   January 1, 1977

   October 14, 1942

   July 4
   (*Not* July 4th but July Fourth; likewise, January first and October fourteenth)

2. Addresses:

   5747 Giddings Street, Chicago, Illinois 60091

   Room 2335, 1600 Market Street,
   San Francisco, California 94102

Apt. 34, The Grandeur Hotel,
600 Granville Avenue,
New York, New York 10022

3. Telephone numbers:

    415-346-8105

    592-6871

4. Hours and minutes used with A.M. or P.M.:

    4:00 P.M.

    8:00 A.M.
    (Not 8 o'clock; rather eight o'clock)

5. Decimals:

    98.6°

    3.1416

6. Certain travel information:

    Highway 80 is one of our finest freeways.

    TWA flight 134 boards at gate 51.

7. Certain data about books:

    The information can be found in paragraph 12
    (lines 8–10) on p. 260 of *Rhetoric in a Modern
    Mode.*

8. All other numbers that cannot be written as
    one or two words:

ORIGINAL	REVISION
She was *19* on February 24, 1971.	She was *nineteen* on February 24, 1971.
General Mung reported that *three thousand five hundred and sixty-two* enemy tanks had been destroyed by his invading troops.	General Mung reported that 3,562 enemy tanks had been destroyed by his invading troops.

Exception

Do not begin sentences with numerals.

ORIGINAL

800 students enthusiastically applauded his last lecture.

REVISION

Eight hundred students enthusiastically applauded his last lecture.

If necessary, rewrite the sentence in order to avoid beginning it with a numeral:

ORIGINAL

2615 Park Blvd. was his address in those years.

REVISION

His address in those years was 2615 Park Blvd.

O

org

Organization—Organize each formal essay so that there is a systematic order of events, details, and ideas.

Since the paragraph can be treated as an essay in miniature, you can greatly improve the organization of your essays by studying the following approach to the organization of the paragraph. In addition, you will find that many of your problems with organization lie in poorly organized paragraphs within the body of the essay itself.

1. Natural order:

For some subjects use natural order. There are two kinds of natural order: *the order of space* and *the order of time.*

(a) The Order of Space

Whenever an assignment requires that you describe a concrete object—a statue, a room, the cover of a magazine, a landscape—your subject contains a natural arrangement: *the order of space.* A room, for instance, can be described in a clockwise or a counterclockwise direction; from the inside or the outside; from the center or a corner; from a fixed or a moving point; from the floor to the ceiling. A person can be described from head to foot; from foot to head; from a central point to either extremity. In other words, *the order of space shows how elements are related to each other in space; such order is built into assignments requiring that you describe things or people.*

Look at a simple example first. The next paragraph uses the order of space to arrange details in the description of a person; it begins with the head and concludes with the feet of the subject— a clear, rather mechanical approach. Because the details are put in climactic order, the organization is also interesting:

I began to believe that teachers are human beings—with human *weaknesses*—when I saw Professor Frog. As he walked into Biology 10 that first morning, I thought, "Good grief—he dresses that way *deliberately.*" Even then I knew the thick red hair couldn't really be his own. I followed it with my eyes as it crawled slowly towards his left ear. Then I took stock of the rest of him. He was wearing an electric-blue sport coat with high padded shoulders. He also wore a vest, in shocking magenta, buttoned haphazardly over a little-girl-pink tie that sparkled with game birds and cattails. His banana-yellow trousers came almost to the tops of his tennis shoes, but there was space enough there for me to see that the orange sock on his right foot didn't quite match the green one on his left foot.

Then look at a more complex example: A. E. Hotchner's description of Ernest Hemingway. Hotchner scans Hemingway's appearance in this order: pants, belt, shirt, shoes, hair, and mustache. Next, in some detail, he describes the dominant impression: Hemingway was "massive." Finally, Hotchner concludes with a much more important point: Hemingway "radiated" *enjoyment*. Despite the complexity of this paragraph, the arrangement of details is both interesting and clear:

> Hemingway . . . was wearing khaki pants held up by a wide old leather belt with a huge buckle inscribed GOTT MIT UNS, a white linen sport shirt that hung loose, and brown leather loafers without socks. His hair was dark with gray highlights, flecked white at the temples, and he had a heavy mustache that ran past the corners of his mouth, but no beard. He was massive. Not in height, for he was only an inch over six feet, but in impact. Most of his two hundred pounds was concentrated above his waist: he had square heavy shoulders, long hugely muscled arms (the left one jaggedly scarred and a bit misshapen at the elbow), a deep chest, a belly-rise but no hips or thighs. Something played off him—he was intense, electrokinetic, but in control, a race horse reined in. He stopped to talk to one of the musicians in fluent Spanish and something about him hit me—*enjoyment*: God, I thought, how he's *enjoying* himself! I had never seen anyone with such an aura of fun and well-being. He radiated it and everyone in the place responded. He had so much more in his face than I had expected to find from seeing his photographs.
>
> —A. E. Hotchner, *Papa Hemingway* (New York: Random House, 1966, p. 6)

(b) The Order of Time

Less frequently you will meet subjects with another kind of natural order—*the order of time.*

When you are asked to write a narrative, a story, or an anecdote, you will need to use the order of time—to show how things happened one after another *in time.* To do that, simply describe what happened, selecting details for interest, of course, and using words like *first, next, then,* and *finally* to show the chronological relationship of events.

Here is a beautiful example: George Orwell's story of shooting an elephant. The elephant, temporarily mad, had killed a native; and as a member of the Indian Imperial Police, Orwell had the job of finding the beast and killing him. He writes:

> When I pulled the trigger I did not hear the bang or feel the kick—one never does when a shot goes home—but I heard the devilish roar of glee that went up from the crowd. In that instant, in too short a time, one would have thought, even for the bullet to get there, a mysterious, terrible change had come over the elephant. He neither stirred nor fell, but every line of his body had altered. He looked suddenly stricken, shrunken, immensely old, as though the frightful impact of the bullet had paralyzed him without knocking him down. At last, after what seemed a long time—it might have been five seconds, I dare say—he sagged flabbily to his knees. His mouth slobbered. An enormous senility seemed to have settled upon him. One could have imagined him thousands of years old. I fired again into the same spot. At the second shot he did not collapse but climbed with desperate slowness to his feet and stood weakly upright, with legs sagging and head

dropping. I fired a third time. That was the shot that did it for him. You could see the agony of it jolt his whole body and knock the last remnant of strength from his legs. But in falling he seemed for a moment to rise, for as his hind legs collapsed beneath him he seemed to tower upwards like a huge rock toppling, his trunk reaching skywards like a tree. He trumpeted for his first and only time. And then down he came, his belly towards me, with a crash that seemed to shake the ground even where I lay.

—George Orwell, "Shooting an Elephant,"
Shooting an Elephant and Other Essays
(New York: Harcourt Brace Jovanovich, 1945)

Remember, then: *to organize a narrative, use the natural order—the order of time.*

2. Logical order:

Besides the natural orders of space and time, there is only one other kind of clear organization: *logical order.*

Logical order simplifies complex ideas and gives shape to formless impressions; it reduces a chaotic swirl of thoughts to a smooth and intelligible flow of connected ideas. It is the essential ingredient of good expository prose.

For most subjects, you can use one of three kinds of logical order: *analysis, classification, comparison-contrast.*

(a) Analysis

Analysis is the process of dividing a whole into its parts; it is a way of "loosening up" anything to separate it into its basic elements or internal divisions.

The following paragraph, for example, analyzes the three main characteristics of the "typical" teen-ager. Notice how the topic sentence lists each

of these characteristics, and how each is taken up
in its proper order in the body of the paragraph.
Notice also that the writer develops a brief
discussion of each part in his analysis:

> It seems to older adults that the typical
> teen-ager today has three main characteristics:
> *he's affluent, he's educated, he's casual about
> sex.* First of all, the teen-ager is affluent: he
> has a *lot* of money to spend. Recent statistics
> show, for instance, that each year teen-agers
> are now spending $570 million on toiletries,
> $1.5 billion on entertainment, and $3.6 billion
> on women's clothes alone. All together, they
> spend close to $12 billion. The typical teen-
> ager is also educated—at least better than
> his parents were. More teen-agers go to school
> and stay there than ever before. In 1900 only
> 13 percent of them were enrolled in school;
> now about 95 percent of them are in high
> school, and about half of those will go to
> college. A third striking characteristic of the
> typical teen-ager is that he's casual about sex.
> This is hard to prove, but it's rather neatly
> illustrated by a story I read in a recent issue
> of *Time:* as a practical joke, a 16-year-old boy
> calmly announced at the dinner table that his
> girl friend was pregnant. Before his shocked
> parents could say anything, his 13-year-old
> brother reacted. "My God," he said. "You'll
> lose your allowance." So, although individuals
> certainly vary, the typical teen-ager seems to
> have three main characteristics.

(b) Classification

Another common and useful kind of logical order
is *classification. Classification works by sorting
things into groups.* It is so closely related to
analysis that it is sometimes seen as an aspect of
the same process, but there is a difference. While
analysis divides a whole into its parts, classifica-

tion brings together similar things to show what they have in common. You will understand the difference if you first analyze and then classify something—a book, for instance. If you *analyze* a book, you take it apart in some systematic way; if you *classify* a book, you place it in a category with other books. For example, if you *analyze* Ian Fleming's *Thrilling Cities,* you can find that it is divided into thirteen chapters, each dealing with one or more cities. But if you *classify* the same book, you can group it with other travel books—Boswell's *Journal of a Tour to the Hebrides* and Arthur Frommer's *Europe on 5 Dollars a Day,* perhaps.

Note that in the following paragraph, the two categories in the classification are explicitly announced in the topic sentence. Each category is then discussed fully in the body of the paragraph.

Words derived from proper nouns fall into two distinct categories: *words that have their origin in the names of individuals and words that develop from place names.* Words in the first category often come from mythology or literature. Take only one example—*procrustean,* from the name of Procrustes, the mythical highwayman who robbed travelers and then placed them on a special bed. If they were too short for the bed, he stretched them out; if they were too long, he cut them off. Hence, *procrustean:* "tending to produce conformity—often by violent means," as in "the *procrustean* schools of America." Words in the second category come from the names of places that for some reason or another have stamped their impression on history. *Sybaritic* is an excellent example: it comes from the name of an ancient Greek city in Southern Italy, Sybaris, whose inhabitants were notorious for a strange mixture of human passions. Sybaritic men loved horses, drunken parties, and other men. They were (almost literally) sitting ducks for their savage neighbors, who coveted the Sybarites' horses and didn't hesitate to slit a few thousand Sybaritic throats in order to get them. So the neighbors got the horses and the Sybarites left only their name to history. To this day *sybaritic* conjures up an image of the person who loves luxury and pleasure—in a slightly effeminate way. Although these two examples don't begin to suggest the wonderful variety of words derived from proper nouns, they aptly illustrate the categories: words that have their origin in the names of individuals and words that develop from place names.

(c) Comparison-Contrast

A third kind of logical order is *comparison-contrast. Comparison points out similarities; contrast points out differences.* Often, however, we use both comparison *and* contrast to organize a discussion of things that are different in some ways and similar in others. For the sake of convenience—and because they have much in common—let's speak of the three processes as *comparison-contrast.*

Use *comparison* to analyze two (or more) things at one time in order to show their *similarities.*

Use *contrast* to analyze two (or more) things at the same time in order to show their *differences.*

Use *comparison-contrast* to analyze two (or more) things that are *different* in some ways and *similar* in other ways.

The Paragraph of Comparison. Study the following paragraph as an example. It comes from an essay entitled "James Bond: Culture Hero," by George Grella. Grella's thesis is that Bond's popularity rests not on his competence as a hero (actually, Bond is incredibly *incompetent)* but on the resemblance of the Bond novels to "historic epic and romance, based on the stuff of myth and legend." In the following paragraph Grella compares the situation in the novel *Moonraker* with the myth of "Perseus-St. George"*:

> In *Moonraker* [by Ian Fleming] the situation parallels the Perseus-St. George myth, an appropriate one for Bond's rescue of London from the great rocket of Sir Hugo Drax, the huge dragon menacing England. Drax has red hair, an ugly, burned face which even plastic surgery cannot mask, splayed "ogre's teeth"; the great burst of fire he hopes to turn on London is the modern equivalent of the dragon's flames. Fleming employs an ironic reversal of one aspect of the Perseus myth; instead of rescuing Andromeda from the cliff where she is chained; Bond and his Andromeda, Galatea Brand, are nearly killed when one of the Dover cliffs, with some urging from Drax, falls on them. Of course Bond survives and, after escaping steamhosing and the liftoff of the Moonraker rocket (more fire from the dragon's nostrils), saves London. Alone among Bond novels, the hero fails to get the girl at the end: as a modern St. George, it would scarcely be appropriate for him to win the fair maiden.
>
> —George Grella, "James Bond: Culture Hero" (*The New Republic,* May 30, 1964)

The Paragraph of Contrast. Use contrast to analyze two (or more) things at the same time in order to show their differences, as in the following paragraph contrasting European and

---

*Perseus, in Greek mythology, was the son of Zeus and Danaë and slayer of the wicked Medusa. He married Andromeda after rescuing her from a sea monster (dragon). St. George, patron saint of England, saved a king's daughter from a dragon (according to legend). This story, it is widely believed, may have been "borrowed" from the story of Perseus' battle with the monster that threatened Andromeda. In myth and legend the two stories are often connected.

American cities. The main idea, stated in the first
sentence, lists three important differences. Each of
these differences is taken up in turn in the body
of the paragraph:

> European cities—French cities in particular—
> are crowded in ways American cities are
> not: most buildings are multi-story; no room
> is left between buildings; and buildings
> are flush with the sidewalk. First, most
> buildings are multi-story. In cities such
> as Paris, Chartres, even places as small as
> Avalon, it is hard to tell a residence from an
> office building. Buildings are three, four, five
> stories at least, especially if they contain
> apartments—which the French often buy as
> homes. There seem to be no one-story
> dwellings such as we so commonly see in
> residential areas in the U.S. Secondly, each
> building is flung right up against the next:
> there is not even room for a passageway. In
> Paris one can walk for blocks without seeing
> daylight except in the "canyons"—the streets
> themselves. It doesn't matter whether it's a
> residential or business area. In America,
> however, most residential and business areas
> offer at least a little open space. Finally, there
> are no lawns and very few trees in front of
> European buildings: they are flush with the
> sidewalk. Most houses in America, of course,
> are set back from the street and the sidewalk,
> leaving room for grass, trees, or some other
> form of greenery. While it is true that fine
> architecture may be enough to compensate for
> lack of space and greenery, it is interesting to
> note that given any excuse, the typical
> Parisian flees to the country: as one of them
> put it, "The trees, the greenery, the space—ah,
> you Americans are so very fortunate."

The Paragraph of Comparison and Contrast.
Use comparison and contrast to analyze two (or
more) things that are different in some ways, and
similar in other ways.

Here is an excellent example—a paragraph that
compares *and* contrasts our now-departed
"hippies" with the subculture that came before
them, the "beats." The main idea, again, is stated
in the first sentence: "there has been a startling
transformation in bohemia." The first sentence
leads into a brief discussion of *similarities*
between hippies and beats; these similarities are
developed in a few details. The third sentence
introduces a discussion of the *differences;* these
are developed in several details. Again, there is no
summary sentence, but the pattern closely
resembles that of the model paragraph of analysis.

> The immediate progenitors of the hippies
> were the beats of the 1950s, but there has
> been a startling transformation in bohemia.
> Many of the same elements were present in
> the beat generation: scorn for prevailing
> sexual mores, a predilection for pot and
> peyote, wanderlust, a penchant for Oriental
> mysticism on the order of Zen and the Veda.
> Yet the contrasts are even more striking. San
> Francisco's North Beach was a study in black
> and white; the Haight-Ashbury is a crazy quilt
> of living color. Black was a basic color in the
> abstract-expressionist painting of the beats;
> hippiedom's psychedelic poster art is
> blindingly vivid. The progressive jazz of the
> beats was coolly cerebral; the acid rock of the
> hippies is as visceral as a torn intestine.

—"The Hippies" *(Time,* July 7, 1967, p. 20)

*Arranging Details in Comparison-Contrast
Paragraphs.* In paragraphs organized by
comparison-contrast, place your details in one of
two ways: *"point-by-point"* or *"block-by-block."*

Suppose for example that you are contrasting European and American cities. You can discuss the differences between them point-by-point, or you can discuss European cities in one part of your paragraph and American cities in the next. You might make a rough outline showing the arrangement of details in each of these two plans:

POINT-BY-POINT ORGANIZATION

European cities	multi-story buildings
American cities	many single-story buildings
European cities	usually no room between buildings
American cities	usually some room between buildings
European cities	buildings flush with sidewalk
American cities	buildings set back from sidewalk

BLOCK-BY-BLOCK ORGANIZATION

European cities	multi-story buildings usually no room between buildings buildings flush with sidewalk
American cities	many single-story buildings usually some room between buildings buildings set back from sidewalk

In writing the paragraph organized point-by-point, you would discuss one point at a time, dealing with European cities in one sentence (or more) and with American cities in the next sentence(s). Look back at the model paragraph to see how that is done.

The paragraph organized point-by-point is usually clearer and sharper, but the paragraph organized block-by-block is by no means uncommon. Suppose for example that you are contrasting the culture of the Pueblo Indians with that of the Dobus (who live on the Dobu Island off the coast of New Guinea). In writing a paragraph organized block-by-block, you would discuss the Pueblos in the first part of the paragraph and the Dobus in the next part, like this:

>　According to Ruth Benedict in *The Patterns of Culture,* the Pueblo Indians are different from the Dobus in three important ways. Take the Pueblos first. The Pueblos have a very cooperative, peaceful society. They are not jealous about sexual rights and they do not punish infidelity. Moreover, they make no display of political or economic power. The Dobus are different in every way. To begin with, they are violent, aggressive people. Unlike the Pueblos, they are intensely jealous: the in-laws spy on married people constantly, and any infidelity is met with swift, brutal punishment. Also, the Dobus are fiercely . proud of political and economic success: like the old-time Captains of American Industry, they worship and will go to any extreme— including fraud and murder—to get what they want.

By now you should see for yourself which of the two arrangements works best: differences (or similarities) are sharper and clearer when the details are arranged point-by-point. *For most comparison-contrast paragraphs, then, use a point-by-point arrangement.*

p

p //　　　**Parallel Structure**—Use parallel grammatical
constructions for ideas parallel in thought.

Parallel means "closely agreeing in essential
qualities and characteristics." Grammatical
constructions are parallel when they have a
likeness or similarity that permits them to be
labeled with the same grammatical tag: "noun
clauses"; "prepositional phrases"; "present
participles." Ideas are parallel when they have
striking similarities or striking differences. Note
that parallel ideas are often joined by
"correlative" conjunctions or other "correlative"
words, such as *both . . . and, not only . . . but
also, not . . . but, either . . . or, neither . . . nor,
some . . . others,* and *the one . . . the other.* Such
words are called "correlative" because they
"co-relate": they convey natural, reciprocal
relationships between the ideas and between the
constructions that contain the ideas.

1. Maintain parallel structure in a series of words, phrases, or clauses:

Words.

ORIGINAL

Riding, swimming, and *the library* made camp fun as well as profitable. (In this series, *the library* is not parallel with the two gerunds *riding* and *swimming.)*

REVISION

Riding, swimming, and *reading* made camp fun as well as profitable. (The three gerunds are parallel.)

Phrases

ORIGINAL

We walked everywhere in Paris that summer—*through the parks, across the bridges of the Seine, down the broad boulevards,* and *ate at sidewalk cafes. (Ate at sidewalk cafes,* a verbal phrase, is not parallel in grammar or in thought to the prepositional phrases to which it is attached.)

REVISION

We walked everywhere in Paris that summer—*through the parks, across the bridges of the Seine, down the broad boulevards,* and *past sidewalk cafes,* where we often stopped to eat escargots and to watch the other walkers. *(Past sidewalk cafes,* a prepositional phrase, is now parallel in thought and grammar to the other prepositional phrases in this sentence. The adjective clause that follows is grammatically correct; it simply adds another idea to the sentence.)

Clauses

ORIGINAL

The sun rose early, we crawled out of our tents, and *on some days all the way to the creek. (On some days all the way to the creek* is not a clause; in grammar and in thought it is not parallel to the other two elements in this sentence.)

REVISION

The sun rose early, we crawled out of our tents, and then *we dashed down to the creek,* though on some days we felt like crawling. *(We dashed down to the creek,* a main clause, is now parallel in grammar and thought to the other main clauses in this sentence. The adverb clause that follows is grammatically correct; it simply adds another idea to the sentence.)

2. Sometimes use parallel structure for rhetorical effect:

Parallel structure is the basic poetic technique of Hebrew poetry; its use takes the place of the rhyme and accentual rhythm that characterize most other poetry, such as English and American verse. As a poetic device, parallel structure can be used occasionally with great force in English prose. Consider, for example, the following passage from Dr. Johnson's famous letter to the Earl of Chesterfield, written in February of 1755, just after Dr. Johnson had published his great *Dictionary*. Chesterfield, who had been cold and distant when Johnson had first approached him, was now offering to be Johnson's "patron." Johnson rejected the offer in the following terms, using parallel phrases most effectively: "Is not a Patron, my Lord, one who looks with unconcern on a man struggling for life in the water, and, when he has reached ground, encumbers him with help? The notice which you have been pleased to take of my labours, had it been early, had been kind; but it has been delayed *till I am indifferent, and cannot enjoy it; till I am solitary, and cannot impart it; till I am known, and do not want it.*"

3. Sometimes use parallel structure to achieve unity and coherence:

As a device of repetition, parallel structure can be used occasionally to achieve unity and coherence. In his "Inaugural Address," delivered January 20, 1961, President John F. Kennedy approached a vast subject—his hope for the future of mankind—and handled it with deceptive ease by setting up a number of parallel series. He begins one group of paragraphs in the following ways:

"To those old allies. . . ."

"To those new states. . . ."

"To those peoples. . . ."

"To our sister republics. . . ."

"To that world assembly of sovereign states. . . ."

"Finally, to those nations. . . ."

He begins another group of paragraphs thus:

"So let us begin anew. . . ."

"Let both sides explore. . . ."

"Let both sides, for the first time, formulate. . . ."

"Let both sides seek. . . ."

"Let both sides unite. . . ."

"And if a beachhead of cooperation may push back the jungle of suspicion, let both sides join. . . ."

The parallel structure and the repetition give the "Inaugural Address" unity and coherence—and force—that the President could have achieved in no other way.

Caution: A common error in parallel structure involves comparisons. For example:

"I am *taller* than *anyone* in this room."

Logically, that statement is absurd, since the speaker, who is presumably in the room himself, cannot be taller than *anyone* in the room: he can only be taller than *anyone else* in the room.

In comparisons, then, *exclude the things compared from other members of the group:*

ORIGINAL	REVISION
Jane is prettier than *any* girl I know. (This statement is illogical, unless the speaker does not know Jane at all.)	Jane is prettier than *any other* girl I know.

paren

Parentheses—Use parentheses only when you want to separate certain parenthetical elements from the rest of the sentence.

One of three devices can be used to set off parenthetical elements: commas, which provide normal separation; dashes, which provide the most emphatic separation; and parentheses, which provide less emphatic separation. Parentheses also have certain special functions.

1. Use parentheses for clearly emphatic clauses and phrases that you feel require distinct separation from the rest of the sentence:

> She admired the dress (though at the moment a mere thirty hung in her closet) and asked if she might try it on.

2. Use parentheses to set off dates, references, and figures in an enumeration:

Dates

Harriet Martineau (1802–1876), an English visitor, wrote complimentary things about American manners as she found them in 1832.

References

Organizing a paragraph is no difficult thing if you know what you are doing (see *Rhetoric in a Modern Mode,* Ch. 3).

Figures in an Enumeration

Her husband charged her with three responsibilities: (1) keeping house; (2) keeping the children out of trouble; (3) keeping up intellectually with him.

Caution: Punctuate in and around parentheses correctly.

(a) Use appropriate end punctuation within the parentheses if the first word begins with a capital letter:

> P. T. Barnum was the king of humbug and the creator of hoaxes. (But he wrote that it is debt that robs a young man of self-respect.)

(b) Use semicolons, colons, and commas when they are necessary after the second parenthesis. Do not use them before it or before an opening parenthesis except in enumeration:

ORIGINAL

There was algae growing in the bottle (which had been filled at Walden Pond;) as a result, the bottle made a strange-looking paperweight.

Richard Henry Dana, Jr., had well-developed antislavery feelings (he legally sought to prevent the return of at least two runaway slaves:) he was determined to thwart the Fugitive Slave Law.

REVISION

There was algae growing in the bottle (which had been filled at Walden Pond); as a result, the bottle made a strange-looking paperweight.

Richard Henry Dana, Jr., had well-developed antislavery feelings (he legally sought to prevent the return of at least two runaway slaves): he was determined to thwart the Fugitive Slave Law.

Note: For the use of question marks in parentheses to cast doubt, see **Question Mark.** For related but distinctly different marks of punctuation, see **Brackets** and **Dash.** Note in particular that brackets most often enclose editorial comment; that dashes emphasize parenthetical material; and that parentheses de-emphasize such material.

pass   **Passive Constructions**—Avoid passive constructions whenever possible.

Passive constructions are subject-verb combinations in which the subject is acted upon by an agent that may or may not be identified after the verb:

PASSIVE	ACTIVE
This *book was written* by Irwin Shaw.	*Irwin Shaw wrote* this book.
It has been announced that *classes will be dismissed* for the rally.	The *president has announced* that *he will dismiss* classes for the rally.
My shoes were shined while I waited.	*The attendant shined* my shoes while I waited.

Like impersonal constructions, passive constructions are not *bad*—they are weak: instead of *acting*, the subject *is acted upon*. Passive constructions are also wordy, simply because they demand more words than active constructions. Finally, since passive constructions may omit the agent, they are vague: often we do not learn who performed the action.

A significant point? It is especially significant in expository and argumentative writing: passive constructions permit—or sometimes encourage—the writer to shun his responsibility to be specific and authoritative. "It is well known that . . ." may sound persuasive, even though the assertion has no substance to it. "The fact has been widely acknowledged that . . ." may not state a fact at all.

In other words, passive constructions are weak, vague, evasive, disingenuous, and often underhanded—if not actively dishonest. Do not use them unless you must.

(See **Impersonal Construction** and **Sentence Structure/Style**.)

p

Period—Use a period at the end of most sentences and non-sentences, for decimals, after abbreviations, and for ellipsis dots.

1. Use a period at the end of declarative and imperative sentences and sentences that ask indirect questions:

Declarative Sentence

The shortest route to San Simeon is Highway 1.

Imperative Sentence

Drive forward to the first pump for quicker service.

Indirect Question

She asked if he could drive her to San Francisco.

2. Use a period after non-sentence salutations and answers to questions:

Good morning.

Hello.

Where are we going? To the supermarket to get steaks for our barbecue.

3. Use a period for decimals:

The ratio of the circumference of a circle to its diameter, known as pi (π), is a transcendental number having a value, to eight decimal places, of 3.14159265.

On this campus you can obtain only 3.2 beer.

4. Use a period after abbreviations:

Mr. Snippet

Mrs. Whilk

N.Y.

Do not, however, use a period after *Miss* (which is not an abbreviation), or after the abbreviations (initials) of many agencies, institutions, and organized groups (FBI, CIA, UNESCO, NAACP).

(See **Abbreviations.)**

5. Use periods for ellipsis marks.

(See **Ellipsis.**)

6. Always place the period *inside* quotation marks, whether the period belongs to the quoted part or to the sentence as a whole:

> I have just finished reading Chekov's great story "The Kiss."

(See **Quotation Marks.**)

q

q   **Question Mark**—Use the question mark when you ask a direct question or in parentheses when you want to express doubt or uncertainty.

Direct Question

Did you lock the door?

Do you have enough money for your date?

You promised to have this paper in on time, didn't you?

Doubt or Uncertainty

The brilliant (?) speaker alternately annoyed and bored his audience.

Wallace Stevens' poem "The Emperor of Ice-Cream," written in 1923 (?), uses symbolic figures to suggest the vulgar inevitability of death.

Note: If the question occurs as part of a quotation, or in the form of a quotation, place the question mark *within* the quotation mark.

ORIGINAL

"Is the plane on schedule," she asked?

REVISION

"Is the plane on schedule?" she asked.

If the entire sentence is a question, however, place the question mark at the end of the sentence, *after* the quotation mark.

ORIGINAL

Did you hear him say, "I'll be home by two o'clock?"

Have you read Chekhov's story "The Kiss?"

REVISION

Did you hear him say, "I'll be home by two o'clock"?

Have you read Chekhov's story "The Kiss"?

---

quot

Quotation Marks—Use quotation marks around all direct quotations from printed material; all quoted dialogue; and the titles of short stories, brief poems, songs, essays, reviews, book chapters, and unpublished manuscripts.

In general, there are two types of quotations: *direct* and *indirect*. The direct quotation sets off the exact words of the speaker or the writer in quotation marks. The indirect quotation, however, is a paraphrase of those words, often introduced by the word *that* (which may be either expressed or implied).

DIRECT

I asked, "How long has she been dead, Bruno?"

"I don't know," he said.

INDIRECT

I asked Bruno how long she had been dead.

He said (that) he didn't know.

1. Use quotation marks around all direct quotations from printed material:

> In *The Rambler* No. CCVII, for Tuesday, March 10, 1752, Samuel Johnson wrote: "Such is the emptiness of human enjoyment, that we are always impatient of the present. Attainment is followed by neglect, and possession by disgust; and the malicious remark of the Greek epigrammatist on marriage may be applied to every other course of life, that its two days of happiness are the first and the last."

Note: Long, formal quotations like this one are introduced by colons; shorter, less formal quotations are introduced by commas.

(See Colon, Comma, and Dialogue.)

2. Use quotation marks to set off quoted dialogue:

> I got close enough to him to smell the garlic and red wine and to see that, as usual, though he looked as though he had not shaved in two days, he had cut himself very recently with a razor. I got really close—close enough to see the open pores in the big nose, and the little red eyes, and the big ears up tight against the greasy dark hair.
>
> I said, "You're crazy, Bruno!"
>
> "Lieutenant, you bore me," he said. "Go scare some kiddies."

(a) Be careful not to omit the second set of quotation marks:

> "I'm leaving right now," she said.

> "I do not object to your language," I said, "but I do object to your ideas."

(b) Always place the verb of saying *outside* the quotation marks:

> She said, "I'll do exactly as I please."

> "I'll do exactly as I please," she said.

> "I'll do," she said, "exactly as I please."

(c) Use commas to set off the verb of saying:

> I said, "Shut up!"

(Compare the indirect quotation: *I said that he should shut up.*)

> "The same to you," he replied.

> "I can't do it," I said, "but you can."

(d) When the verb of saying comes after the quoted dialogue, do not use a comma if the quotation itself ends in a question mark or an exclamation point:

> "Shut up!" he said.

> "Oh, won't you?" I asked.

(Note that the sentence itself ends with a period.)

(e) The verb of saying is sometimes omitted:

> "Do you love me?"

> "Of course, darling! What do you take me for?"

> "I don't know. . . . Sometimes I'm so unsure."

(f) Written dialogue represents the directly quoted speech of usually two or more persons talking together. It is standard practice, however, to write each person's speech, no matter how short, as a separate paragraph. Related bits of narration, including verbs of saying, are customarily presented in the paragraph along with the speech.

> There was a long pause.
> "Is that all?" Alice timidly asked.
> "That's all," said Humpty Dumpty. "Good-bye."

This was rather sudden, Alice thought: but, after such a *very* strong hint that she ought to be going, she felt that it would hardly be civil to stay. So she got up, and held out her hand. "Good-bye, till we meet again!" she said as cheerfully as she could.

"I shouldn't know you again if we *did* meet," Humpty Dumpty replied in a discontented tone, giving her one of his fingers to shake: "you're so exactly like other people."

—Lewis Carroll, *Through the Looking-Glass*

(See **Dialogue** for a discussion of dialogue per se.)

3. Use quotation marks around the titles of short stories, brief poems, songs, essays, reviews, book chapters, and unpublished manuscripts:

Short Stories

"Of This Time, of That Place," by Lionel Trilling, is one of my favorite stories.

Brief Poems

Have you read Gene Fowler's poem "The Words"?

(But: Milton's *Paradise Lost* is certainly a long poem.)

Songs

"White Christmas" is maudlin but still rather nice.

Essays (reviews, book chapters, and other brief prose compositions)

I have just finished reading Edgar Allan Poe's "The Poetic Principle."

(See **Italics.**)

Note: When using quotation marks, be sure to place other marks of punctuation correctly.

The rule is simple. Periods and commas always go *inside* the quotation marks. Colons, dashes, and semicolons always go *outside* the quotation marks. Exclamation points and question marks go inside the quotation marks if they are part of the quoted material; otherwise, they go outside the quotation marks:

Period

For tomorrow, read James Lynn Barton's poem "To a Lady in My Arms."

Comma

For tomorrow, read "To a Lady in My Arms," which was written by James Lynn Barton in 1967.

Colon

For tomorrow, read "To a Lady in My Arms": it provides a perfect antidote to the genteel, squeamish gloom of "The Love Song of J. Alfred Prufrock."

Dash

For tomorrow, read, "To a Lady in My Arms"—by James Lynn Barton—and come prepared to contrast it with "The Love Song of J. Alfred Prufrock."

Semicolon

For tomorrow, read "To a Lady in My Arms"; we will compare and contrast it with "The Love Song of J. Alfred Prufrock."

Exclamation Point

He shouted, "Bizarre!"

Look at those "creeps"!

Question Mark

Have you read "To a Lady in My Arms"?

We are going to discuss the question "Is there life after death?"

Note also: for a quotation within a quotation, use an "inverted comma" for a "single" quotation mark (') as opposed to a "double" quotation mark ("):

> "The smell down below was as unexpected as it was frightful. One would have thought hundreds of paraffin lamps had been flaring and smoking in that hole for days. The man with me coughed and said, 'Funny smell, sir.' I answered negligently, 'It's good for the health, they say,' and walked aft."
>
> —Joseph Conrad, "Youth"

---

ref

Reference (of pronouns)—In general, use no pronoun that lacks a definite antecedent.

1. Each pronoun should point clearly to its antecedent (the noun it replaces); the reference should never be vague and indefinite:

ORIGINAL

At the store I was told *they* were out of French bread and mushrooms. *(They* has no antecedent; it refers vaguely to the proprietors of the store.)

In the morning paper *it* said that the killer of six coeds had been captured. *(It* has no definite antecedent.)

REVISION

At the store I was told by the clerk that *he* was out of French bread and mushrooms. *(He* clearly refers back to its antecedent, *clerk.)*

A story in the morning paper said that the killer of six coeds had been captured. (The pronoun *it* has been replaced by the noun *story.)*

2. Do not use a pronoun to refer to an entire preceding sentence, clause, or phrase:

ORIGINAL

Finance charges usually add hundreds of dollars to the purchase price of a car. *This* should be taken into consideration in computing the total cost. *(This refers vaguely to the idea expressed in the entire first sentence.)*

REVISION

Finance charges usually add hundreds of dollars to the purchase price of a car. This *fact* should be taken into consideration in computing the total cost. *(This is now used as a demonstrative adjective modifying fact.)*

3. Avoid ambiguous pronoun reference:

Ambiguous pronoun reference occurs when a pronoun might refer to any of several persons or things. When the reference is ambiguous, the entire sentence needs to be rewritten to make the reference clear.

ORIGINAL

Bob told John *he* needed to get *his* hair cut. After all, Martha and Judy were going to the dance too, and *their* appearance was important. (Who needed a haircut, Bob or John? Whose appearance was important? The antecedents of *he, his,* and *their* are ambiguous.)

(See **Shift/Point of View.**)

REVISION

Bob told John, "*I* need to get *my* hair cut. After all, Martha and Judy are going to the dance too, and our appearance is important." *(I* and *my* clearly refer to Bob. *Our* clearly refers to Bob and John. The pronoun reference is no longer ambiguous.)

rep

Repetition—Do not thoughtlessly repeat sounds, words, ideas, or sentence patterns.

Many kinds of repetition make artful, effective writing, especially when the writer uses repetition with some conscious aim in mind. Thus alliteration—the repetition of initial sounds of words—is a poetic device occasionally used in writing prose. The repetition of important words establishes continuity, coherence, and unity. The repetition of ideas can emphasize an important point. But thoughtless repetition of sounds, words, ideas, or sentence patterns stands out like crumbs on a beard.

The following examples are typical of careless, ineffective repetition:

Sounds

A *part* of my *heart* loved her, but my *mind* was *blind* to her *charms*, even when I held her in my *arms* and stared at the *swarms* of golden specks to be *seen* deep in her *green* eyes. (Rhyme, we can probably agree, makes prose sound like bad verse.)

Words

Next would be growth. It is hard to say that this could be called a *reality* of life, but one must admit that it is *real*. This is an easy *reality* to *realize* because growing I am doing. (We are not sure what this means. But the repetition makes it sound sillier and emptier than it *really* is.)

Ideas

Thurber's essay is one of entertainment for his readers, also giving vent to his pet peeves. That is just exactly what it is, pure enjoyment to read in a satirical fashion. It is an entertaining essay about the life of a typical college student. Actually, this subject is a difficult one to write about. . . . (Yes, indeed. This student had nothing to say on the assigned subject, so he says it three times—in the hope that verbosity will resemble substance —before he admits that he has nothing to say.)

Sentence Patterns

The cat walked along a branch. The dog sat under the tree. I stood on the sidewalk. I wondered what would happen next. (Do not make every sentence a brief, staccato statement, beginning with the subject and verb. Vary your sentence structure slightly.)

(See Sentence Structure/Style.)

---

rt

Run-Together Sentences—Do not write two or more independent clauses as one sentence.

There are three cars in my garage none of them is very new.

This statement is a run-together sentence because it consists of two separate main clauses joined without appropriate punctuation or conjunctions. Closer examination shows that, in actuality, the run-together sentence is really two sentences:

There are three cars in my garage.
None of them is very new.

You may correct run-together sentences in any of several ways—but do *not* make the correction at random. Think intelligently about it. The way you choose should depend on the sentences themselves, the rhythms you feel are appropriate, and the context of the surrounding sentences.

1. Correct some run-together sentences by separating the main clauses with a period.

(See Period.)

ORIGINAL

I love Sue however it is unlikely I will marry her. *(I love Sue* is a main clause. It should be set off from the other main clause.)

REVISION

I love Sue. However, it is unlikely I will marry her.

2. Correct some run-together sentences by separating the main clauses with a semicolon.

(See Semicolon.)

ORIGINAL

I like to look at the mountains they are very beautiful at this time of the year. *(I like to look at the mountains* is a main clause. It should be set off from the other main clause.)

REVISION

I like to look at the mountains; they are very beautiful at this time of the year.

3. Correct some run-together sentences by joining the main clauses with a comma and a coordinating conjunction *(and, or, nor, but, yet, for).*

(See Comma.)

ORIGINAL

The food was good the service was execrable. *(The food was good* is a main clause. It should be set off from the other main clause.)

REVISION

The food was good, *but* the service was execrable.

4. Correct some run-together sentences by subordinating one clause and using appropriate comma punctuation.

(See **Comma** and **Subordination.**)

ORIGINAL

I like to work in the sun I have to be very careful not to get sunburned, however. *(I like to work in the sun* is a main clause. It should be set off from the other main clause.)

REVISION

Although I like to work in the sun, I have to be very careful not to get sunburned. (The main clause *I like to work in the sun* has been subordinated—that is, linked to the other main clause by a subordinate conjunction, *although,* and set off by comma punctuation.)

S

semi

Semicolon—Use the semicolon to separate two or more closely related independent clauses not joined by a coordinating conjunction; use the semicolon for rhetorical effect; use the semicolon, as required, to prevent confusion.

1. Use the semicolon to separate two or more closely related independent clauses not joined by a coordinating conjunction:

> Ted slept on the floor; she retired to the roof.

> The cat leaped into my arms; the raccoon, puzzled, stared curiously at us both.

Note:
(a) The coordinating conjunctions in English are *and, or, nor, but, yet,* and *for.*
(b) The semicolon in the construction may be replaced by a comma plus a coordinating conjunction:

> Ted slept on the floor, *but* she retired to the roof.

(c) In a long, complicated sentence, the semicolon may also be used *with* a coordinating conjunction:

> Sometimes, after long hours of writhing in pain and loneliness, she felt like putting an end to it all; *but* then she remembered Bob and clung tenaciously to her hope, for she knew that, no matter what, he loved her, even though he had kicked out all her teeth.

> "A shrewd peasant was always well enough protected against imposters in the market place, and we have all sorts of businessmen who have made themselves excellent judges of phoniness without the benefit of a high-school diploma; *but* this kind of shrewdness goes along with a great deal of credulity."
>
> —Alan Simpson, "The Marks of an Educated Man" (*Context,* I, No. 1, Spring 1961)

(d) The semicolon is most frequently used to join two main clauses connected rhetorically by a conjunctive adverb. (Conjunctive adverbs are words like *however, nevertheless, consequently, then, thereupon, moreover, therefore, hence, furthermore, besides.* They show transitions in thought, but they do not link clauses grammatically. See **Comma Splice.**)

> Ted slept on the floor; *however,* she retired to the roof.

> The cat leaped into my arms; *then* the raccoon, puzzled, stared curiously at us both.

Note, first, that the conjunctive adverb is generally set off by a comma; and, secondly, that the conjunctive adverb (unlike true conjunctions) can be readily moved to other positions in the clause:

> Ted slept on the floor; she, *however,* retired to the roof.

> Ted slept on the floor; she retired to the roof, *however.*

2. Use the semicolon for rhetorical effect:

Occasionally the semicolon can be used with great effectiveness to link together a series of short main clauses:

> A quarter moon is still up; the eastern sky is pink behind the rim of mountains; but black clouds lie on them to the south, and the morning is still dark over the lights of Redwood City; birds sing; down in the park, a lone rooster crows; sunrise comes to my silent room, atop my little hill; it is now 5:10 A.M.

3. Use the semicolon to prevent confusion in constructions which, like the following, require internal comma punctuation:

> In Paris that year I knew Martha St. John, who wrote dirty poetry and got filthy drunk on two glasses of wine; Jonathan Wild, who was later arrested for attacking the Eiffel Tower with a war-surplus bazooka, screaming, "I'll get you, you bloody Martians!"; and Gilmore Stern, an apoplectic young painter who lived in a huge, drafty studio with two scrawny models and a pack of greyhounds.

Note: always place the semicolon *after* a quotation mark:

> For tomorrow, read "To a Lady in My Arms"; we will contrast it with "The Love Song of J. Alfred Prufrock."

SS

Sentence Structure/Style—Make each sentence as effective as possible in its context; prefer the plain style.

One learns to write well by writing and rewriting so diligently and carefully that the fitting word, the just construction, the perfectly appropriate rhythm comes with its own polished, natural eloquence. To a few writers such strength and ease require only the effort of lifting a pen or flicking graceful fingers over the keys of a singing typewriter. Most of us, however, must work at writing—work hard, with little advice, or no advice, or bad advice, which is unspeakably worse than no advice. And as your writing matures, you'll probably discover for yourself that most of the advice you've been given was bad advice, given by people who either don't write at all or write badly, and hence compounded of ignorance, prejudice, and mindless devotion to tradition, qualities molded by obstinancy and confusion into a set of *Rules for Writing Well.* Forget it. Most of what you've been taught under that rubric is tainted: it is unadulterated rubbish.

1. Correcting faulty sentence structure (see *Awkward Phrasing*):

When a sentence goes astray—and comes back marked *SS* for *Sentence structure/Style*—you can only try to improve it by rewriting it. Make it *sound* correct, using your natural sentence sense as you cut and add words, shift phrases and clauses. No set of rules can tell you exactly what to do, since each bad sentence is bad in its own special way; it bears the stench of corrupt individuality; and it must be cleaned and polished to an immaculate uniqueness. For example:

ORIGINAL	REVISION
Johnny Cash, one of America's greatest Western musicians, and who is extremely popular among young people because of his political and social sympathies, is a great live performer, one who can charm and thrill any audience. (The first *and* does not belong in this sentence; *sympathies* is not quite the right word; *greatest* followed by *great* makes awkward repetition; the two appositive constructions introduced by *one* and the two adjective clauses introduced by *who* are extremely awkward as they are yoked together in this sentence.)	Johnny Cash, a great Western musician who is extremely popular among young people because of his political and social views, is an excellent live performer, able to charm and thrill any audience. (The sentence is still perhaps too long: the idea expressed by the adjective clause probably needs to be developed and emphasized in a separate sentence.)
I like *Playboy* because of its fine articles and interesting stories, and it always has a good variety of beautiful women pictured in various stages of natural beauty. *(Beauty* following *beautiful* is awkward. The second clause could be better expressed as a phrase; and note that its circumlocutions suggest that the writer is embarrassed by what he is saying.)	I like *Playboy* because of its fine articles, its interesting stories, and its good variety of beautiful women depicted more or less naked.

2. Improving your sentence structure:

As Socrates said, "Agree with me if I seem to speak the truth." For it seems to us there *are* devices of style that you can use systematically to improve the sentence structure of everything you write, from love letters to essay examinations. We offer this brief discussion of such devices, however, not as a set of rules but as a series of suggestions; you may either accept or reject them. George Orwell, in "Politics and the English Language," has stated the basic principle: "If you simplify your English, you are freed from the worst follies of orthodoxy."

(a) *Prefer the short sentence to the long.*
That is not to say that you should write in a "Dick-and-Jane" style, but that short sentences are direct, powerful, and easy to write. They have strength and force. They have the natural dignity of the spoken language. And they are much more readable.

(b) *Vary the length of your sentences.*
The first objection to short sentences is that they are dull, flat, and choppy. But only when used carelessly. There are two answers to this objection, then: *first,* turn some of your short sentences into longer ones by joining the main clauses with proper punctuation—semicolons, colons, and dashes—so that your sentences *seem* longer, even though most of your ideas are still stated in brief main clauses; *secondly,* achieve the effect of variation by writing some extremely short sentences and some rather long ones. Shift rhythms. The result will not be dull, flat, choppy sentences, but zestful, pungent, cadenced prose.

(c) *Begin most sentences with the subject and the verb.*
The natural sentence in English today is the "cumulative" sentence, which (like this one) begins with the subject and verb of the main clause and adds modifying clauses and phrases if necessary, so that ideas "accumulate" to cling to the main statement. An occasional subordinate clause, prepositional phrase, or participial construction at the beginning of a sentence does no harm; in fact, judiciously used, it may even interject a spirited, unanticipated shift in rhythm, improving the movement of an entire passage. But

do *not* use such constructions very often: you'll
send your reader bouncing through a clatter of
variation—of gerunds, gerundives, participles,
noun and adverb clauses, prepositional phrases—
until his head spins and his teeth ache.

Elegant variation, as it is usually taught, will
poison your style.

(d) *Use a familiar vocabulary.*
Let us quote H. W. Fowler in *The King's English:*

> Anyone who wishes to become a good
> writer should endeavor, before he allows
> himself to be tempted by the more showy
> qualities, to be direct, simple, brief, vigorous,
> and lucid. This general principle may be
> translated into practical rules in the domain of
> vocabulary as follows:—
>
> > Prefer the familiar word to the farfetched.
> > Prefer the concrete word to the abstract.
> > Prefer the single word to the
> > circumlocution.
> > Prefer the short word to the long.
> > Prefer the Saxon word to the Romance.
>
> These rules are given roughly in the order
> of merit; the last is also the least.

In giving similar advice in "Politics and the
English Language," George Orwell aptly sums up
for us this discussion of sentence structure and
style:

> (i) Never use a metaphor, simile or other
> figure of speech which you are used to seeing
> in print.
>
> (ii) Never use a long word where a short
> one will do.
>
> (iii) If it is possible to cut a word out,
> always cut it out.
>
> (iv) Never use the passive where you can
> use the active.

(v) Never use a foreign phrase, a scientific word or a jargon word if you think of an everyday English equivalent.

(vi) Break any of these rules sooner than say anything outright barbarous.

(See **Awkward Phrasing, Subordination,** and **Wrong Word.**)

---

shf/pv　**Shift/Point of View**—Do not shift carelessly from one point of view to another: use one pronoun consistently in order to maintain a single point of view.

ORIGINAL

I like to get up very early when I am forced to write something. You can think most clearly in the morning, and the earlier I get up, the more I get accomplished. (The writer should not shift from I to you: he should maintain one point of view consistently.)

A student must prepare for *his* final exams. *You* will not get far without adequate preparation. (*You,* the second person pronoun, is carelessly used here to refer to the second person pronoun, *his,* which in turn refers back to *student.*)

(See **Reference.**)

REVISION

I like to get up very early when I am forced to write something. I can think most clearly early in the morning, and the earlier I get up, the more I get accomplished.

A student must prepare for *his* final exams. *He* will not get far without adequate preparation. (The third person pronouns *his* and *he* now are used correctly to refer to *student.*)

shf/t

Shift/Tense—Stick consistently to one verb tense. Do not change tenses unnecessarily.

In telling a story, writing an anecdote, or summarizing a writer's argument, use one verb tense consistently. For plot summaries in particular, use the *present* tense; the convention for doing so is firmly established.

ORIGINAL

In Sophocles' *Oedipus Rex*, Oedipus *learns* that he *has killed* his father and *married* his mother, Jocasta. When he *found* this out, he *tore* a pin from Jocasta's dress—after she *had hanged* herself—and *stabbed* out his eyes. At the end of the play, he *walks* away blind, banished from his kingdom. (In the first and third sentences, the writer uses the present and present perfect tenses. In the second sentence, however, he shifts to the past and past perfect tenses, thereby distorting the time-angle from which he views events.)

(See **Tense.**)

REVISION

In Sophocles' *Oedipus Rex*, Oedipus *learns* that he *has killed* his father and *married* his mother, Jocasta. When he *finds* this out, he *tears* a pin from Jocasta's dress—after she *has hanged* herself—and *stabs* out his eyes. At the end of the play, he *walks* away blind, banished from his kingdom. (Now the present and present perfect tenses are used consistently. Note that the present perfect tense—as in *has hanged*—is used for past events as they are viewed from the present.)

sp

Spelling—Spell each word correctly. Carefully correct every error in spelling. Learn the basic rules of English orthography (correct spelling), and master a list of frequently misspelled words.

Although the poor speller seldom fails to communicate his meaning clearly, he may alarm and annoy his reader, creating a mistrust so keen that the reader rejects the writer's perceptions and ideas along with his misspellings.

Certain good habits characterize the work of a

good speller. The good speller consults a dictionary for the correct spelling of every doubtful word. No experience, no rules, can take the place of a recent college desk dictionary. The good speller also uses his memory-system—eyes, ears, hands—in studying the spelling of a difficult word: he *looks* at the word and notes its syllabification; he *pronounces* the word so that he hears it with fidelity; he *writes* it more than once to mark its shape in the muscles and nerves of his hands. His practice is to look, hear, write.

Besides using a dictionary, the good speller knows a few basic rules of spelling—and is familiar with many of the exceptions to the rules.

English orthography by its very nature admits many exceptions. Before learning any rules, then, you should thoughtfully consider some of the factors that are responsible for the difficulties of English spelling. First, the dissemination of printed books, beginning about 1500, tended to fix the spelling of English words even though their pronunciation continued to change. In the word *knight,* for instance, the silent *k* and *gh* were once pronounced. Second, English vocabulary is made up of a high percentage of foreign words, and their etymology tends to influence their spelling. Third, our alphabet of twenty-six letters is simply inadequate to represent systematically the twenty-one vowel sounds and twenty-five consonant sounds of twentieth-century American English. Finally, as Mario Pei points out in *The Story of English* (Fawcett World Library: New York, 1952, pp. 280-81), a tremendous variety of letters may be used to represent a single sound—there are fourteen possible ways to spell the *sh* sound—or, conversely, we may get a number of different sounds out of one combination of letters, such as the seven different sounds represented by *ough (dough, bought, bough, rough, through, thorough,* and *hiccough).* In short, as Pei says, "English spelling is the world's most awesome mess" (p. 280).

Spelling Rules

To eliminate some of the difficulties of English spelling, you should learn the following five rules, which are regular enough to be useful:

1. *Doubling the final consonant.* When a word ends with a single consonant preceded by a single vowel, *double* the final consonant before a suffix beginning with a vowel if the base word has only one syllable, or if the base word is accented on the last syllable.

Note the three elements in this complex rule:

(a) The base word must end with a single consonant preceded by a single vowel, as in *begin, stop, occur, prefer.*

(b) The base word must have only one syllable or be accented on the final syllable, as in *big, drop,* and *brag,* or in *deFER, exPEL,* and *reFER.*

(c) The suffix must begin with a vowel, as in *-ar, -er, -ess, -ed,* and *-ing.*

Examples (base word + consonant + suffix):

adMIT	+	t	+	ed	=	adMITTed
beGIN	+	n	+	ing	=	beGINNing
comPEL	+	l	+	ing	=	comPELLing
deFER	+	r	+	ed	=	deFERRed
fog	+	g	+	y	=	foGGy
stop	+	p	+	ed	=	stoPPed

Note: do not double the final consonant if it is preceded by more than one vowel: *appear, appeared, appearance.* Do not double the final consonant in words ending in silent *e: write, writing; come, coming; dine, dining.* (An obvious exception is *write, written:* in *written* the spelling changes to accommodate the change in pronunciation, as the long *i* of *write* becomes the short *i* of *written.*)

2. *I before e*. When the sound is *ee*, write *i* before *e* except after *c*; otherwise write *e* before *i*. A useful mnemonic (memory) device is the rhyme

> Write *i* before *e*
> Except after *c*,
> Or if sounded like *a*
> As in *neighbor* or *weigh*.

Examples
(*i* before *e*
except after *c*)   (after *c*)   (sounded like *a*)

belief	perceive	veil
grief	ceiling	reign
pierce	receive	freight
yield	receipt	vein

Exceptions: *either, neither, weird, forfeit, leisure, seize, species, height, foreign.*

3. *Dropping the silent e*. When a word ends in a silent *e*, drop the *e* when you add a suffix beginning with a vowel; keep the *e* when you add a suffix beginning with a consonant.

Examples (suffix beginning with a vowel):

admire	+	able	=	admirable
bite	+	ing	=	biting
create	+	ive	=	creative
fame	+	ous	=	famous
mange	+	y	=	mangy

Exceptions: words ending in *ce* or *ge* usually retain the *e* to preserve a soft *c* or *g* sound, as in *advantageous, changeable, outrageous,* and *noticeable.* Variant spellings are also possible—and equally correct: *movable, moveable; likable, likeable; lovable, loveable.*

Examples (suffix beginning with a consonant):

care	+	ful	=	careful
life	+	like	=	lifelike
advertise	+	ment	=	advertisement
complete	+	ly	=	completely

Exceptions: *wholly, argument, judgment, truly, awful.*

4. *Changing y to i.* When a word ends with a consonant + *y*, change the *y* to *i* when you add a suffix. Usually do not change the *y* if the suffix begins with *i*.

Examples (consonant + y + suffix):

baby	+	es	=	babies
baby	+	ing	=	babying
				(suffix begins with *i*)
busy	+	ly	=	busily
defy	+	ance	=	defiance
forty	+	eth	=	fortieth
happy	+	er	=	happier
lobby	+	ed	=	lobbied
likely	+	hood	=	likelihood
marry	+	age	=	marriage
weary	+	ness	=	weariness

Exceptions: *dryness, dryly; shyly, shyness; slyly, slyness; wryly, wryness.*

Note: when the final *y* is preceded by a vowel instead of a consonant, do not change the *y* to *i*, as in *buy, buyer; employ, employment; play, played.*

Exceptions: *daily, gaiety, paid, said.*

5. *Adding prefixes.* Do not change the basic spelling of a word when you add prefixes such as *un-, mis-,* or *dis-.*
Examples:

discharge

disenchanted

misspell

misunderstood

unhappy

unnecessary

Spelling List

The following words are frequently misspelled by college students.* When you have mastered these words, you will have eliminated many of your personal spelling difficulties.

accept	attendance	coming
achieve	author	comparative
acquire	basically	conceive
adolescence	beginner	conscience
advice	beginning	conscious
advise	belief	consider
all right	believe	consistent
analysis	beneficial	controversial
analyze	benefited	criticism
apparent	Britain	criticize
appearance	business	curriculum
arguing	capital	dealt
argument	category	decide
arithmetic	choose	definite
article	chose	definition
athlete	clothes	dependent

*Based on a study of spelling by college students made by Thomas Clark Pollock ("Spelling Report," *College English,* November 1954).

describe
description
despair
disastrous
disease
effect
embarrass
environment
equipped
exaggerate
excellent
except
existence
fallacy
foreign
forty
friend
fulfill
government
grammar
guarantee
guidance
hear
height
here
heroes
heroine
hypocrisy
independent
influential
intelligent
interest
its (possessive pronoun)
it's (contraction = it is)
laid
led
leisure
lives

lonely
loose
lose
maintenance
mathematics
mere
mischief
necessary
Negroes
ninety
noticeable
noticing
obstacle
occasion
occurred
occurrence
opinion
opponent
optimism
origin
paid
parallel
particular
passed
past
performance
permanent
personal
personnel
persuade
piece
possess
possession
possible
practical
precede
preferred
prejudice
prepare
prevalent

principal
principle
privilege
probably
procedure
proceed
professor
psychology
pursue
quantity
quiet
quite
realize
receive
recommend
referring
relieve
repetition
rhyme (variant: rime)
rhythm
rising
sacrifice
seize
sense
separate
sergeant
shepherd
similar
sophomore
speech
subtle
success
surprise
temperament
than
their
themselves
then
there
therefore

they're	weird	write
to	where	writer
too	whether	writing
tragedy	whole	written
tries	who's (contraction = who is)	yield
two		your (possessive pronoun)
vacuum	whose (possessive pronoun)	you're (contraction = you are)
villain	woman	
weather		

sub

Subordination—Subordinate less important ideas by placing them in dependent clauses clearly related to the main clause or clauses of the sentence.

Since some ideas are much more important than others, you will want to emphasize those ideas by stating them in main clauses. But such emphasis is difficult to achieve if you express *every* idea in consecutive main clauses or coordinate clauses. To emphasize important ideas, then, and at the same time to convey proper relationships between ideas, *subordinate* less important ideas by placing them in dependent clauses or in phrases, or by expressing them as one word if possible.

1. Subordinate (dependent) clauses:

ORIGINAL

Some notable sight was drawing the passengers to the windows. I rose and crossed the car to see what it was. (Each idea receives the same emphasis; that is, each is placed in a main clause. No relationship of ideas is conveyed.)

REVISION

Because some notable sight was drawing the passengers to the windows, I rose and crossed the car to see what it was. (The idea in the first clause is now subordinate: it has been placed in a dependent clause introduced by *because.* In addition to shifting the emphasis to the second clause, the new arrangement establishes a cause-and-effect relationship.)

Coach Wilson expects to have a winning team this season. He is in his second year. (Neither idea receives proper emphasis, and no significant relationship is fixed between the two ideas.)

Coach Wilson, *who is in his second year,* expects to have a winning team this season. (The second sentence, now a nonrestrictive adjective clause, is properly subordinated to the first, since it merely adds some extra information.)

2. Phrases:

ORIGINAL

He was failing his classes. He was fatigued. He had been working forty hours a week at his job. He decided to quit school. (The short, choppy sentences give emphasis to none of the ideas.)

REVISION

Failing his classes and fatigued from working forty hours a week at his job, he decided to quit school. (The subordinate ideas are expressed as phrases, while the most important idea is stated in the main clause.)

3. Words:

ORIGINAL

The car was old, and it was in bad need of repair.

REVISION

The *old* car was in bad need of repair. (The first clause is replaced by the adjective *old.*)

t

Tense—Make the tense of each verb agree with the time of the action. Do not carelessly shift from one tense to another.

1. Use the correct tense for each verb:

He *arrives* by plane. (present tense)

He *arrived* by plane. (past tense)

He *will arrive* by plane. (future tense)

2. Shift verb tense only when the time of the action shifts:

He *cashed* the check and *spent* the money. (The time of the action does not shift; thus the verbs are both in the simple past tense.)

Because he *failed* his calculus course last spring, he *cannot qualify* for the summer job at Lockheed. (The action in the subordinate clause is prior to the action of the main clause. There actually *is* a shift in the time of

action from past to present. Thus the shift
from the past tense *failed* to the present tense
cannot qualify is correct and proper.)

Note: For further discussion of shifts in the tense
of verbs, see **Shift/Tense.**

3. Use the present tense for something that is
always so:

Many travelers have said that San Francisco *is*
a city of breathtaking beauty. *(Is,* not *was.)*

ti

Titles—Make your titles relevant and interesting.

Your titles should be relevant to the subject of
your essay, obviously; most titles are. But your
title should also be interesting; most titles aren't.
They are flat, dull, and insipid. Try harder. Use
your imagination.

ORIGINAL	REVISION
"My Trip to Las Vegas"	"Las Vegas (What?) Las Vegas (Can't Hear You! Too Noisy) Las Vegas!!!!"
"Little-known Facts about America's Favorite Indoor Recreational Activity"	"The Sex-Life of the Bowling Ball"
"Comparison and Contrast of Three Attitudes toward Love"	"Love Comes in Strange Packages"
"A Day in the Park"	"A Perfect Day for Plastic Kites"

Note: follow standard editorial practice in the
treatment of titles.

1. Center the title of your own paper in capital letters. If you have a separate title page, center your title in capital letters halfway down the page:

INSIDE PRUFROCK

On the first page of your essay, drop down about one-third of the page and center your title and name thus:

INSIDE PRUFROCK

by

James Barton

2. Place the titles of shorter works, when you name them, in quotation marks. When you refer to the title of an essay, story, or poem—any part of a longer work—place the title in quotation marks:

> In Susan Glaspell's story "A Jury of Her Peers," there is an ironic reversal in the roles of men and women.

(See **Quotation Marks.**)

3. Italicize the titles of any longer works when you refer to them. Italicize (underline) the titles of novels, plays, books of nonfiction, movies, and television programs:

> *The Great Gatsby* deals with the American Dream.

> *Hamlet* is one of the world's best-known plays.

> I regularly watch *All in the Family.*

(See **Italics.**)

ts

Topic Sentences—Use the topic sentence to state the main idea of your paragraph.

A topic sentence works by doing two things: first, it lays down your subject; secondly, it puts forth your main idea about that subject. We can say, then, that a topic sentence has two parts: a *subject;* and something said about that subject, which we can call the *focus.* For example:

SUBJECT:	FOCUS:
education	. . . is very important in the modern world
drama	I like . . .
music	. . . is interesting and enjoyable

A good topic sentence has a *limited* subject and a *sharp* focus. A limited subject clearly marks off your specific material; a sharp focus points out *exactly* what you will say about that material. A weak topic sentence, by contrast, has a broad subject and a vague focus; such a sentence leads nowhere in particular—except to a loose, poorly unified, badly developed, disorganized paragraph.

ORIGINAL

Music is interesting and enjoyable. (This topic sentence has a broad subject—music—and a vague focus.)

REVISION

Folk-rock appeals mainly to the younger generation. (This topic sentence represents an improvement because the subject is limited to a specific kind of music and the focus is sharper.)

The San Francisco sound combines the rhythms of rock-and-roll with the lyrics of the folk ballad. (This topic sentence is better still because the subject is more limited and the focus is much sharper. The writer has now committed himself to writing about *the San Francisco sound* instead of about *music* generally, and he must show that the San Francisco sound does something quite specific: it *combines the rhythms of rock-and-roll with the lyrics of the folk ballad*.)

Modern innovations have revolutionized life.

(See **Unity**.)

Power tools such as the circular saw have made framing a house easier and faster than ever before.

---

tr

Transitions—Use transitional devices to show your reader how your ideas fit together—that is, to help you achieve continuity in your writing.

Transitions are like bridges: they carry your reader across the gaps between sentences and paragraphs. Find the meaning in the etymology: *trans*, "across"; *-ition*, "going"; *trans-ition*—"going across." *So a transition is a word or a phrase that connects ideas. Within the paragraph, transitions show how sentences are tied to each other and to the main idea.*

Learn to use three common transitional devices:

1. Pronoun reference

2. Repetition of important words

3. Transitional expressions

1. First, learn to use pronoun reference to achieve continuity:

Take the following paragraph as an example of the way pronouns can be used to tie sentences together in the paragraph. Here, Susanne K. Langer

begins with the topic sentence "Of all born creatures, man is the only one who cannot live by
bread alone." In the rest of the paragraph Langer
gets continuity by using the word *he* (and its
variants *his* and *him*) to refer back to *man*. Note
that the pronoun appears at or near the beginning
of most of the sentences, and that there is never
any doubt about what word the pronoun refers
back to:

> Of all born creatures, man is the only one that
> cannot live by bread alone. *He* lives as much
> by symbols as by sense report, in a realm
> compounded of tangible things and virtual
> images, of actual events and ominous portents,
> always between fact and fiction. For *he* sees
> not only actualities but meanings. *He* has,
> indeed, all the impulses and interests of
> animal nature; *he* eats, sleeps, mates, seeks
> comfort and safety, flees pain, falls sick and
> dies, just as cats and bears and fishes and
> butterflies do. But *he* has something more in
> his repertoire, too—*he* has laws and religions,
> theories and dogmas, because *he* lives not
> only through sense but through symbols. That
> is the special asset of *his* mind, which makes
> *him* the master of earth and all its progeny.
>
> —Susanne K. Langer, "The Lord of Creation"
> (*Fortune Magazine*, January 1944)

2. Second, learn to repeat important words to
achieve continuity:

In one shining paragraph from his essay "The
Culture of Machine Living," Max Lerner gets
continuity by repeating the word *standardized* (as
well as by using clear pronoun reference). He has
placed his topic sentence at the end of the
preceding paragraph: "Someone with a satiric
intent could do a withering take-off on the rituals
of American standardization." Now, he writes:

> Most American babies . . . are born in
> *standardized* hospitals, with a *standardized*

tag put around them to keep them from getting confused with other *standardized* products of the hospital. Many of them grow up in uniform rows of tenements or suburban houses. They are wheeled about in *standard* perambulators, shiny or shabby as may be, fed from *standardized* bottles with *standardized* nipples according to *standardized* formulas, and tied up with *standardized* diapers. In childhood they are fed *standardized* breakfast foods out of *standardized* boxes with pictures of *standardized* heroes on them. They are sent to monotonously similar schoolhouses, where almost uniformly *standardized* teachers ladle out to them *standardized* information out of *standardized* textbooks. . . .

> —Max Lerner, "The Culture of Machine Living," *America as a Civilization* (New York: Simon & Schuster, 1957)

But that is, after all, a *tour de force*, a highly polished display of technical virtuosity—and you are not very likely to want to imitate its methods. For a more practical example of the way word repetition can be used to tie sentences together, look closely at this paragraph: it gets continuity by repeating the words *changes, won,* and *controversy:*

We have witnessed widespread *changes* in society and in the lives of women. These *changes* from the earlier status quo have been hard *won* and accompanied by *controversy.* We are still in the midst of *change* and *controversy.* For example, we have *won* recognition of the principles of equality in legal and nonlegal areas. However, we must still work hard at translating these principles into particular actions and, since *change* comes hard, we can expect more *controversy.*

> —Mary Louis McBee and Kathryn A. Blake, *The American Woman: Who Will She Be?* (Beverly Hills: Glencoe Press, 1974, p. 7)

3. Finally, learn to use transitional expressions to achieve continuity:

Transitional expressions are words and phrases that, for the most part, have only one job in the language: to show how events or ideas or things are related to one another. Alone, they mean nothing: these are empty words. Suppose someone walks up to you and says, "In the first place, however, thus, consequently, nevertheless, last!" See?

But as gimmicks and gadgets of language they are most useful. They underline infinitely important relationships; they give you an extraordinarily exact way of showing how sentences in a paragraph are related to the main idea and to each other.

Pull the transitional expressions from this paragraph, for example—and see how little sense is left:

Result: introduces conclusion drawn from preceding paragraphs

Addition: shows how one thing happens after another

Addition: introduces further explanation

Result: introduces conclusion drawn from details in this paragraph

Contrast: introduces contrasting conclusion

Addition: introduces explanation for preceding statement

Addition: introduces further explanation

Thus, in the perspective of biology, war first dwindles to the status of a rare curiosity. Further probing, however, makes it loom larger again. For one thing, it is a form of intra-specific struggle, and as such may be useless or even harmful to the species as a whole. Then we find that one of the very few animal species that make war is man; and man is today not merely the highest product of evolution, but the only type still capable of real evolutionary progress. And, war, though it need not always be so harmful to the human species and its progress, indubitably is so when conducted in the total fashion which is necessary in this technological age, Thus war is not merely a human problem; it is a biological problem of the broadest scope, for on its abolition may depend life's ability to continue the progress which it has slowly but steadily achieved through more than a thousand million years.

—Sir Julian Huxley, "War as a Biological Phenomenon" from *On Living in a Revolution* (New York: Harper & Row, Publishers, 1942)

As you write, then, keep before you this "catalog" of transitional expressions, organized around the relationships they usually bring out:

Addition

additionally, again, also, and also, and then, as well, besides, beyond that, equally important, first (second, third, fourth, finally, last, lastly, *etc.*), for one thing, further, furthermore, in addition, likewise, moreover, next, now, on top of that, over and above that

Comparison

in the same way, likewise, similarly

Contrast

after all, although this may be true, and yet, be that as it may, but, even so, for all that, however, in contrast, in other circumstances, in spite of that, nevertheless, nonetheless, on the contrary, on the other hand, otherwise, still, yet

Emphasis

above all, certainly, especially, in any event, in fact, in particular, indeed, most important, surely

Exemplification

as an example, as an illustration, for example, for instance, in other words, in particular, that is

Place

above that, at this point, below that, beyond that, here, near by, next to that, on the other side, outside, within

Reason

for this purpose, for this reason, to this end

Result

accordingly, as a consequence, as a result, consequently, for that reason, hence, inevitably, necessarily, that being the case, then, therefore, thus

Summary

as has been noted, as I have said, finally, in brief, in other words, in short, in sum, lastly, on the whole, to be sure, to sum up

Time

after a while, afterward, at last, at length, at once, briefly, by degrees, eventually, finally, first (second, third, *etc.*), gradually, immediately, in a short time, in the future, in the meantime, instantaneously, later, meanwhile, promptly, soon, suddenly

4. In most paragraphs, mix your transitional devices: combine pronoun reference, repetition of important words, and transitional expressions to achieve the most effective continuity:

The reason for the mixture is quite simple: repetition dulls, but variety sharpens, interest. Look at the next paragraph, for example, where the writer balances pronoun reference *(we, us, our)*, repetition of important words *(teen-agers, teen-years, teens)*, and transitional expressions *(for instance, on the other hand)*—to get continuity *and* interest.

Pronoun
(referring
back to
teen-agers)

Pronoun

Transitional
expression

Pronoun

Transitional
expression

Important
word

Repetition of
important
word

Pronoun

Repetition of
important
word

Pronoun

And since we [teen-agers] are so new,
many people have some very wrong ideas
about us. For instance, the newspapers
are always carrying advice-columns
telling our mothers how to handle us,
their "bewildered maladjusted offspring,"
and the movies portray us as half-witted
bops; and in the current best sellers,
authors recall their own confused,
unhappy youth. On the other hand,
speakers tell us that these teen-years
are the happiest and freest of our lives,
or hand us the "leaders of tomorrow,
forge on the future" line. The general
opinion is that teen-agers are either car-
stealing, dope-taking delinquents, or
immature, weepy adolescents with
nothing on our minds but boys (or girls
as the case may be). Most adults have
one of two attitudes toward the handling
of teens—some say that only a sound
beating will keep us in line; others treat
us as mentally unbalanced creatures on
the brink of insanity, who must be
pampered and shielded at any cost.

—Judith D. Matz, "The New Third Age"
(*American Judaism*, Winter 1964–65)

In brief, don't make your reader jump desperate-
ly from one idea to another, like a flea changing
dogs; use your transitions to *carry* him across the
gaps between sentences. *Get continuity in orderly
arrangement; point out the continuity with
transitional devices—pronoun reference, repetition
of important words, and transitional expressions.*

tri

Trite Ideas—Do not permit yourself to express trite ideas as though they were fresh, novel, original observations.

Trite ideas are commonplaces—ideas expressed so frequently that they have lost interest and become stale and vapid. They are characterized by wornout expressions, treatments, or points of view. They are platitudes decorated with clichés.

When your instructor marks an idea *trite,* then, he means that you have not thought for yourself in your own language. Such a passage can be revised only by re-thinking and rewriting it in its entirety.

For instance, this trite idea cannot simply be rephrased: "In today's complex world a college education is necessary for success." *In today's complex world* is a cliché; the entire idea itself is, first, commonplace; secondly, obvious; and thirdly, with a little *original* thinking, rather questionable. What is *success,* for example? Happiness? Middle-class suburban bliss behind a white picket fence? Wealth? And why *necessary?* Do *all* successful men have college educations? What about Willie Mays, a "successful" baseball player? What about the Beatles, "successful" musicians?

In other words, trite ideas must be inserted into a mental microscope, scrutinized carefully, and then discarded, once you've recorded your *real* observations. Don't let the world do your thinking —or your writing—for you.

(See **Cliché.**)

u

Unity—Achieve unity by making sure each sentence in your paragraph is directly related to the idea expressed by your topic sentence.

Unity means oneness—and you get it by sticking to your main idea, by making sure every sentence carries its part of the burden instead of drifting off into unrelated ideas.

Take for example the following paragraph. It has unity; it hangs together as a whole. Note that the first sentence states the main idea: "At exam time I learned the sad truth that Americans are at no stage in their career taught how to write." As you read the paragraph, note that the writer explains what happened at exam time to make him come to this opinion. Every sentence turns on this point, his main idea.

At exam time I learned the sad truth that Americans are at no stage in their career taught how to write. I mean this not only in the literary sense but also physically. The student who can type beautifully on his own electric typewriter almost disintegrates when asked to put pen to paper for an hour or two in an examination. The lack of style, the misspelling, and the idiotic punctuation drove me to despair from which I was only rescued by the occasional discovery of first-rate answers and the odd remarks that were unintentionally funny. One student, for example, called Homer's epic "The Achilliad." Another wrote that "St. Augustine was illuminated by divine power." (I had to put the comment, "A.C. or D.C.?") In an essay on the *Song of Roland* a girl wrote: "He charged in against the dragon relying on God to help him, and if He didn't, well that's the way the cookie crumbles." Another girl throughout her answers referred to "sweetie-pie Aristotle."

—Richard Gilbert, "A Good Time at UCLA: an English View" (*Harper's Magazine,* April 1965)

Stick to the main idea and you can't go wrong. This sounds simple enough. But look at how quickly you can stray off into unrelated ideas. Watch what happens as a student argues that we are becoming a nation of cheaters. His first two sentences set up the main idea and give an example to support it—but sentence three catches at *another* idea: the reasons for cheating. This is undoubtedly suggested by the main idea, but it does not carry out the main idea; instead, it drifts off into a little story about last night's "date," splitting the paragraph into two pieces. The sense of unity is lost; the feeling of oneness is broken.

(1) You don't have to look very far to see that just about everyone, in one way or another, cheats, apparently with the approval of their family and friends, which makes them cheaters too. *(2)* For example, my father pads

his expense account every time he goes on a business trip. *(3)* Of course, one of the reasons Americans cheat is that everything is so expensive. *(4)* Just last night I took out a girl who wanted an orchid corsage. *(5)* That was five dollars. *(6)* And then there was the price of the dinner (ten dollars), admission to the dance (four-fifty), and a snack afterwards (four dollars). *(7)* All together, she cost me twenty-three-fifty, but we had so much fun it was worth the money. *(8)* So, like everyone else I cheat too—because I have to.

In short, only sentences 1 and 2 stick to the point; sentences 3–8 skip off into other ideas, and the paragraph loses unity.

To achieve unity, then, you must make absolutely certain that each sentence in your paragraph is directly related to the idea expressed by your topic sentence.

(See **Topic Sentences**.)

---

usg

Usage—For most writing, choose words from the general vocabulary of Standard English: that is, use language appropriate to your subject and your audience.

Standard English is the spoken and written language of educated men and women. Nonstandard English is the language of illiterate people, of certain dialect groups, and of some minorities.

Standard English

Standard English, the linguists tell us, consists of three varieties which shade into one another: Informal English, General English, and Formal English.

1. Informal English

Informal English, more often spoken than written, is the language used by educated people in private conversations, personal letters, and that writing—such as some fiction—intended to be close to popular speech. Informal English is characterized by colloquial words and constructions (such expressions as *goings on, hasn't got, exam,* and *no go,* and contractions like *don't, it's,* and *we'd*) and by slang. Slang is, as Stuart Berg Flexner writes in his *Dictionary of American Slang,* "the body of words and expressions frequently used by or intelligible to a rather large portion of the general American public, but not accepted as good, formal usage by the majority." Slang includes words and expressions such as *goof off, gunk, teenybopper, phony, screwed-up, flip off, son-of-a-bitch, scram, make a scene, jump the gun, enthuse, bum, creep* and *big shot.* Most college desk dictionaries employ usage labels for colloquialisms and slang.

In addition to the special flavor of its vocabulary, Informal English tends to use a less tightly organized sentence structure—a loose structure consisting largely of main clauses standing alone as complete sentences, or joined by coordinating conjunctions to form compound sentences. Just as often, however, Informal English relies on run-together sentences, sentence fragments, and partially completed phrases, supplemented by gestures, facial expressions, and intonation to make meanings clear. Thus the written language, when it attempts to reproduce colloquial English accurately, in actuality simplifies the spoken language by reducing this mélange to printed symbols.

Although some instructors find it acceptable, *as a rule Informal English is not appropriate to college writing.* Hence most errors in usage will require that you change the offending word or construction from Informal (or sometimes Nonstandard) English to General English.

2. General English

General English, both spoken and written, is appropriate to almost any subject or any audience. Its tone may range from the extremely formal to the very informal, but its vocabulary consists largely of those words—*not* labeled by dictionaries—used by educated men and women. Thus General English, in practice, is a literary language, used in business letters, advertising copy, book reviews, written examinations, student essays, professional fiction and nonfiction of all sorts, and an extensive variety of other writing. The constructions employed in General English are those considered "correct" by educated people.

3. Formal English

Formal English, almost exclusively a written language, is characterized by a precise, extensive vocabulary, with a high proportion of words derived from Latin and Greek. It uses a tighter, more complex structure than either of the other two varieties of Standard English. Formal English is appropriate to formal occasions—technical and scientific reports, academic writing, books and articles written for professional groups. It is appropriate to *some* college writing, but it often sounds wooden and stilted, and for that reason perhaps ought to be left to the academics who are coerced by convention into using it, or to the scoundrels who, having nothing to say, take refuge in it.

Nonstandard English

Nonstandard English is the speech of uneducated men and women. It is characterized by socially unacceptable—and therefore "ungrammatical"—constructions such as the double negative ("He don't have none") and by words such as *ain't*. In addition, it uses many words and constructions confined to limited regions. Hence the speech of the ignorant white Southerner differs radically from that of the Pennsylvania Dutch farm boy or the Seattle ghetto child—but all three may speak forms of Nonstandard English.

We want to make it indisputably clear, however, that we do not condemn Nonstandard English as bad English. Both authors of this book grew up speaking varieties of Nonstandard English, one of us as a small-town Texas boy, the other as a street-child in a Chicago ghetto. But as it is the business of colleges and universities to educate men and women, it is also their business to give their graduates a language in which ideas can be discussed with dignity and sophistication. So you must not think that your instructors are assaulting your rightful linguistic heritage—or attacking you personally—when they criticize a usage that comes naturally to you but does not belong to Standard English. They are simply doing their job, a necessary one if you come to college with the best of motives—to acquire an education.

(See Appendix B, **Glossary of Usage.**)

wor

Wordiness—Cut out every unnecessary word.

"Verbosity is a disease," said Sheridan Baker in *The Complete Stylist*. And Gustave Flaubert once advised, "Whenever you can shorten a sentence, do. And one always can. The best sentence? The shortest." Pliny the Younger, we are told, ended a letter by saying, "I apologize for this long letter; I didn't have time to shorten it." Dr. Johnson urged us, "Read over your compositions, and when you meet with a passage which you think is particularly fine, strike it out."

The worst sentences, then, are puffed up with mere words, stuffed with the soft bombast of insubstantial, cottony diction. To write well, cut out the padding. Leave the hard, rigid frame of each sentence.

ORIGINAL

Good and effective writing is not done in accordance with a set of rules with which we guide ourselves, but with taste, intelligence, and sensitivity, which are among the best guides of all. (Be wary of long, empty phrases like *in accordance with*. Watch your *which*-clauses.)

In the fast-moving world of today in which we are faced with many important and significant social problems, not the least of which is the ecological effect on the environment of pollution of the air, land, and waterways in this once-beautiful country in which we live. *(In the fast-moving world of today* is a crutch on which millions of students have hobbled through empty sentences. *In which we live* seems rather obvious—and why repeat it, except in desperation? The *ecology* comprehends the *environment;* certainly both words are not necessary. Avoid passive constructions like *we are faced.)*

REVISION

Good writing is produced not by rules but by taste, intelligence, and sensitivity.

Today we face many important problems; the most important is perhaps the pollution of the air, land, and waterways in this once-beautiful country.

(See **Awkward Phrasing** and **Sentence Structure**.)

ww

Wrong Word—Use each word in its proper sense or senses.

A word marked *Wrong Word* simply doesn't belong: it exists, certainly, but it does not fit into the sentence you have forced it into, as you will see by studying the meanings of the word in any good dictionary. Using the wrong word not only confuses your reader: it obscures your meaning, and it marks your paper with the stamp of ignorance.

Never write without frequently consulting a good dictionary.

ORIGINAL

The *magnanimous* number of homeless, starving people in this country is staggering. (*Magnanimous* does not mean "huge"; it means "courageous, noble, generous.")

Am I going to sign my *unscrupulous* name? (We have not yet determined what this student meant. *Unscrupulous* means "without principles or morality; lacking ideas of right and wrong.")

With the hope of Christ, let us *prey* that Grossmont College will be a huge success. (*To prey* means, basically, "to plunder." Surely the word this student sought was *pray.*)

Intoxicated persons do *rational* acts that they would otherwise avoid. (*Irrational* acts?)

Man is not a *pragmatic* animal; he is *precarious*. (When *two* words are obviously misused, one can only guess at the writer's meaning.)

(See **Awkward Phrasing**.)

REVISION

The *vast* number of homeless, starving people in this country is staggering.

Am I going to sign my *inscrutable* name? (*Inscrutable* means "mysterious, not readily comprehensible." Was that the word this student had in mind? If so, *why?*)

With the hope of Christ, let us *pray* that Grossmont College will be a huge success. (The sentence is not much improved, but at least we are no longer being invited to commit an act of piracy.)

Every book ought to have a conclusion. Let us end our little book, then, with a pregnant, enigmatic observation by one of the ancient wise: "Out of nothing, nothing can come, and nothing can become nothing" (Persius). Good writing!

Appendix A

The Research Paper

Put in the simplest terms, the research paper is a writing assignment, usually requiring research in the library. We say "usually" because materials for such papers may also be acquired from experiments, interviews, speeches, films, and so on. Typically, the research paper is longer than other papers you are asked to write throughout the course. It represents an in-depth treatment of a particular subject, either assigned by the instructor or chosen by you.

Too often students regard the assignment of a research paper as a diabolical plot on the part of their instructors. Such an assignment need not be boring or frightening, however; it can, in fact, be a profitable and enjoyable experience. The research paper can help you with the kind of writing that will be required of you in courses other than English and give you practice in research, organization, and writing methods that will be valuable after you leave school. As you proceed with your paper, it is quite possible that you will enjoy acquiring a degree of expertise in your subject and discovering new insights and relationships.

Choosing the Topic

Unless your instructor assigns a particular subject for your research paper, your first step is to choose a topic. Everyone is interested in something. What interests you? If you are a film buff, you might investigate William Randolph Hearst's reaction to the classic *Citizen Kane*. What do you want to know more about? If you are considering a career in medical technology, you might check on fields of specialization, skill requirements, and so on. Select a topic that you are interested in learning more about. Discuss your choice with your instructor. He or she can probably tell you whether or not the topic is practical in terms of the kind and amount of information available.

Narrowing the Topic

After you have chosen or been assigned a general topic, you will probably need to narrow the subject and to decide strategy—whether the paper is to be argumentative or informational. One good place to start is by looking at general reference works such as encyclopedias—Americana or Britannica for example—under appropriate headings to get a general view of your topic. This may help you decide what facet of the subject you wish to investigate and what your strategy will be.

For example, the course is health education and your topic is cigarette smoking. Quickly you discover that cigarette smoking is linked to a number of maladies such as lung cancer and heart disease. Obviously cigarette smoking is a health hazard. That information is even printed on the package. But why? And here you have a tentative thesis statement, an argumentative thesis statement:

> Cigarette smoking is a health hazard because it is linked to a number of diseases, especially cancer and heart disease.

As your blueprint, such a thesis statement tells you that, after your introduction, the first part of your paper requires that you link cigarette smoking to lung cancer and the second that you link cigarette smoking to heart disease.

Or perhaps you might want to tackle an explanation of what there is about cigarette smoking that does damage. Thus your tentative thesis statement—an informational one this time—might look like this:

> The noxious elements in cigarette smoke consist of tar, nicotine, and carbon monoxide.

Again, the thesis statement provides you with a blueprint for organizing your paper: first an introduction; then a section dealing with tar from cigarette smoke and the damage it does; a second section with nicotine; and a third with carbon monoxide. In any case, the thesis statements above are not fixed or unchangeable: they are tentative. Treat your thesis as a hypothesis, subject to reshaping in the light of new evidence.

The Detective Work

Now find material. First, try the card catalogue in your library. The card catalogue lists each book in the library at least three times: by author's name, last name first; by title of the book; by subject or topic. Your best bet is to look under your topic. Each card usually contains enough information to indicate whether or not the book will be of any use. If it is, list it and all other books you find by call number, author, title, and publication data (publisher, place of publication, and copyright date) on a piece of paper or, better yet, on 4″ × 6″ cards. Take good care of these cards: later much of what is on them will become your bibliography.

For two reasons, it is a good idea not to go to the stacks for your books until you feel your list is complete. First, you'll need to make only one trip. Second, expect at least half the books you want to be checked out of the library. Thus, if some books aren't available, you can simply continue down the shelves in search of the next one on your list *ad nauseam.*

But your list isn't complete until you look at the periodicals. Periodicals are more current. (It usually takes as long to publish a book as it does to have a baby—about nine months.) To find appropriate periodicals, consult the *Reader's Guide to Periodical Literature,* which is published twice each month except during July and August. *Reader's Guide* is alphabetically arranged by author's last name and topic. Once again, your best bet is to search out your topic and the appropriate subheading.

Another index worth looking at is the *New York Times Index,* published twice each month. Over the years, the *New York Times* has been an important resource for most scholars: it is regarded by many as the most reliable day-by-day chronicle of the United States.

There are other indexes, such as the pamphlet file, in which to find leads to useful material. But for these indexes, ask the help of your reference librarians, who always seem to know what is where and how to put one's hands on it. Most reference librarians are eager to help you.

Finally, before proceeding to the next stage—

gathering information from these books, magazines, etc.—ask yourself what might be available in the community. For example, for a paper on abortion, especially one in favor of it, The Planned Parenthood Association, with offices in most communities, is a gold mine of information. If your subject is related to governmental activities, especially on the local level, the local League of Women Voters is a rich source of material. You might get some vital information or references by interviewing local politicians or board members. If the subject is related to the hazards of cigarette smoking or pollution, try the local offices of the American Cancer Society or the American Lung Association. Chances are the publications of these two organizations will either give you the data you need or else indicate where it can be found. Here, again, interviews—if you can get them—with qualified medical personnel such as lung surgeons or heart specialists no doubt will prove useful. In certain situations, the *best* source—perhaps the only source—may be the interview. Such a situation could develop if, for example, you opted to argue in favor of capital punishment. There are few pieces of writing from that side of the issue to match the arguments of opponents such as Michael V. Di Salle or Thorsten Sellin. Under the circumstances, interviews with an assistant district attorney, for example, might turn up useful material. One caution, however: it's not good practice to waste an interviewee's time. Therefore, arrive equipped with knowledgeable questions written out, but be flexible enough to follow up answers that suggest further questions, questions not on your list. Do your best to get accurate notes. With the permission of the interviewee, use a tape recorder.

Note Taking

Use either 3″ × 5″ or 4″ × 6″ cards for notes—
one note per book, magazine article, etc., per card
no matter whether that note be a paraphrase or a
direct quotation. Why only one note per card? For
reasons of organizational flexibility. You will be
shuffling these cards to adjust any organizational
changes you make. Two notes on one card present
a problem: what do you do if one note belongs in
one place in the organizational plan and the second note in another? Secondly, make certain that
each card identifies the source of the material including page number(s). Hint: instead of writing
title and author on each card, assign all entries in
your bibliography a number and simply use these
numbers on your cards for identification.

As you take notes, always be sure to use
quotation marks around directly quoted material.
To avoid the possibility of plagiarism it is a good
idea to take information verbatim from your
sources. In this way you will be able to keep
track of when and how you are rephrasing versus
directly quoting information in your final paper,
without going back to each source.

When you have finished taking notes, organize
your cards into cohesive groups according to the
various points covered. For example, if your topic
is the noxious elements in cigarette smoke, one
stack of cards will deal with introductory material
on what these elements are (tar, nicotine, carbon
monoxide). Another stack will include a
definition, description, etc., of tar; the next stack
nicotine; and so on. If your teacher requires that
you submit an outline for your paper, don't panic.
By sorting and grouping the note cards, you are
creating the basis for an outline.

Footnotes

Footnote all direct quotations. Failure to enclose such material in quotation marks and to acknowledge the source leaves you open to charges of plagiarism.

Some hints about direct quotations:

1. Always provide a lead-in for all direct quotations:

> H. L. Mencken reports that for twenty-six years Edgar Allan Poe's grave was unmarked because "The stonecutter . . . was preparing to haul it [a plain stone] to the churchyard when a runaway freight-train smashed into his stoneyard and broke the stone to bits. Thereafter the Poes seem to have forgotten Cousin Edgar: at all events nothing further was done."[1]

2. Directly quote those opinions or factual details that you want to stand out; paraphrase—put in your own words—everything else so that your paper sounds like you.

3. Use ellipsis points—three periods (. . .) a type space apart—in place of words or whole sentences omitted from a direct quotation either for lack of importance or pertinence as in the first sentence in the example under hint number one.

4. Use brackets to interrupt a direct quotation for an editorial comment. For example, should you come across an error in the material being quoted, insert [*sic*]—"thus it is in the original"—immediately following the error:

> The Livermore *News* reported that "Mrs. Berry is a highly taunted [*sic*] member of Naive [*sic*] Daughters of the Golden West."

---

[1]H. L. Mencken, "Three American Immortals," *Prejudices: A Selection,* ed. James T. Farrell (New York: Vintage Books, 1954), p. 44.

Also use brackets to make an editorial insertion at a given point in the quotation as an aid to clarity. Brackets were used for that purpose in the first sentence of the example under hint number one.

5. For direct quotations of approximately fifty words or more single space, indent margins left and right, and do not use quotation marks.

Where, then, did Poe's tombstone come from? Mencken explains it this way:

> The existing tombstone was erected by a committee of Baltimore schoolmarms and cost about $1,000. It took the dear girls ten long years to raise the money. They started out with a "literary entertainment" which yielded $380. This was in 1865. Six years later the fund had made such slow progress that, with accumulated interest, it came to but $587.02. Three years more went by: it now reached $627.66. Then some anonymous Poeista came down with $100, two others gave $50 each, one of the devoted schoolmarms raised $52 in nickels and dimes, and George W. Childs agreed to pay any remaining deficit. During all this time not a single American author of position gave the project any aid.[2]

Footnote paraphrased material outside the realm of common knowledge. For example, it is common knowledge that Walt Whitman wrote *Leaves of Grass*. But the fact that he was fired in 1865 from his $600-a-year clerk's job in the U.S. Department of the Interior for being a poet is not. Therefore such material should be footnoted. *If in doubt, footnote.*

---

[2]Ibid., p. 45

FORMAT FOR FOOTNOTING

The research paper is based on information or opinions gathered from several sources, and footnotes are your means of giving credit to those sources. While there are many systems of footnoting, the most widely accepted is that established by the Modern Language Association in its pamphlet, *The MLA Style Sheet,* Second Edition.

Numbering

Footnotes are numbered consecutively with Arabic numbers, starting with number 1. These numbers correspond with the numbers assigned to the materials in the text requiring documentation. In the body of the paper the number is placed one-half space above the line and after the material to be footnoted. In the footnote itself, the number precedes the acknowledgement, is indented five spaces, and is placed one-half space above the line.

Placement

Footnotes go at the bottom of the page containing the material to be acknowledged or on a separate page at the end of the paper and before the bibliography. When footnotes are placed at the bottom of the page, they are sometimes separated from the body of the paper by a short line starting at the left-hand margin. Most of the time, however, footnotes begin two spaces below the last line of copy. When footnotes appear at the bottom of the page, they are single spaced, with the first line indented five spaces; double spacing is used between footnotes. When they appear at the end of the paper, they are usually double spaced.

Primary footnotes, those given the first time a source is mentioned, generally contain four components: name of author, title of work, data regarding publication, and page number(s).

Footnote for a book:

> E. R. Hooker, *Study Book in English Literature* (Boston: D. C. Heath, 1910), p. 117.

Footnote for a magazine article:

> Joseph Wechsberg, "Paris Journal," *Gourmet*, April 1975, p. 12.

If the volume number is given, then the symbol "p." or "pp." for page or pages is dropped:

> Hillier Krieghbaum, "Two Gemini Space Flights in Two Metropolitan Dailies," *Journalism Quarterly*, 43, No. 2 (Spring 1966), 120–22.

(Further primary footnotes appear in the section comparing footnote and bibliographical forms.)

Secondary footnotes: After you have used a primary footnote, refer to the same source with a shortened form, usually just the name of the author and page:

> Hooker, p. 117.

If more than one work by the same author is being used, include the title of the work:

> Wechsberg, "Paris Journal," p. 12.

Ibid., an abbreviation of the Latin *ibidem*, "in the same place," is sometimes used to refer to the footnote immediately preceding, *provided both footnotes are on the same page;* otherwise the shortened form (author and page) is used. Thus *Ibid.* means previous source, same page. *Ibid.* plus *p.* means same source but a different page.

> E. R. Hooker, *Study Book in English Literature* (Boston: D. C. Heath, 1910), p. 117.

> Ibid. (or)

> Hooker, p. 117.

If the page number is different:

> Ibid., p. 118 (or)
>
> Hooker, p. 118.

Op. cit. and *loc. cit.*, once employed extensively in secondary footnotes, are unnecessarily confusing and no longer used.

Bibliography

The bibliography is a list of all sources used in the research paper. This includes not only published works, such as books and articles, but interviews and experiments. The bibliography appears as the last item in the research paper. Entries are alphabetized by author's last name. Unlike footnotes, bibliography citations are not indented but begin at the left-hand margin. All subsequent lines are indented five spaces. Entries may be single spaced with double spacing between them or double spaced throughout. Differences and similarities between bibliography and footnote citations are shown in the following section.

Bibliography and Footnote Forms

BOOKS

One author

Bibliography

McKown, Robin. *The World of Mary Cassatt.* New York: Thomas Y. Crowell, 1972.

Footnote

[1]Robin McKown, *The World of Mary Cassatt* (New York: Thomas Y. Crowell, 1972), p. 60.

Two authors

Bibliography

Horowitz, I. A., and Fred Reinfeld. *How to Think Ahead in Chess.* New York: Simon & Schuster, 1964.

Footnote

[2]I. A. Horowitz and Fred Reinfeld. *How to Think Ahead in Chess* (New York: Simon & Schuster, 1964), p. 43.

More than three authors

Bibliography

Bell, James K., et al. *Exploring the Poetry of Gene Fowler.* Berkeley: Obsidian Press, 1974.

Footnote

[3]James K. Bell et al., *Exploring the Poetry of Gene Fowler* (Berkeley: Obsidian Press, 1974), p. 103.

Anonymous author

Bibliography

H.E.L.P.: Home Emergency Ladies' Pal. Canoga Park, Ca.: Xyzyx Information Corp., 1972.

Footnote

[4]*H.E.L.P.: Home Emergency Ladies' Pal* (Canoga Park, Ca.: Xyzyx Information Corp., 1972), p. 42.

Organizational authorship

Bibliography

Exploring Energy Choices. Washington, D.C.: The Ford Foundation, 1974.

Footnote

[5]*Exploring Energy Choices* (Washington, D.C.: The Ford Foundation, 1974), p. 3.

New edition

Bibliography

Stephenson, Ralph, and Jean R. Dedrix. *The Cinema as Art,* 2nd ed. Baltimore: Penguin Books, 1969.

Footnote

[6]Ralph Stephenson and Jean R. Dedrix, *The Cinema as Art,* 2nd ed. (Baltimore: Penguin Books, 1969), p. 89.

Editor(s)

Bibliography

Adelstein, Michael E., and Jean G. Pival, eds. *Women's Liberation.* New York: St. Martin's Press, 1972.

Footnote

[7]Michael E. Adelstein and Jean G. Pival, eds., *Women's Liberation* (New York: St. Martin's Press, 1972), pp. 35–36.

More than one volume

Bibliography

Mack, Maynard, et al., eds. *World Masterpieces.* 2 vols. New York: Norton, 1956.

Footnote

[8]Maynard Mack et al., eds., *World Masterpieces* (New York: Norton, 1956), II, 125.

(Note: After volume number, page symbol—*p.* or *pp.*—is dropped.)

Translation

Bibliography

Serullaz, Maurice. *French Painting: The Impressionist Painters.* Trans. W. J. Strachan. New York: Universe Books, n.d.

Footnote

[9]Maurice Serullaz, *French Painting: The Impressionist Painters,* trans. W. J. Strachan (New York: Universe Books, n.d.), pp. 33–35.

(Note: *n.d.* means no date is included in your source. When no publisher or place of publication is included, use *n.p.* When pages are not numbered, indicate *n.pag.*—no pagination—in place of page numbers.)

Part of a series

Bibliography

Kennard, Jean E. *The Literature of the Absurd.* Harper Studies in Language and Literature. New York: Harper & Row, 1975.

Footnote

[10]Jean E. Kennard, *The Literature of the Absurd.* Harper Studies in Language and Literature (New York: Harper & Row, 1975), p. 12.

Series with editor

Bibliography
Shakespeare, William. *Twelfth Night.* Ed. T. H. Howard-Hill.
Blackfriars Shakespeare. Dubuque: Wm. C. Brown, 1969.

Footnote
[11]William Shakespeare, *Twelfth Night,* ed. T. H. Howard-Hill, The Blackfriars Shakespeare (Dubuque: Wm. C. Brown, 1969), p. 24.

Introduction

Bibliography
Collins, Wilkie. *The Moonstone.* New York: The Heritage Press, 1959.

Footnote
[12]Vincent Starrett, "Introduction," *The Moonstone,* by Wilkie Collins (New York: The Heritage Press, 1959), pp. xiii–xiv.

(Note: In the bibliography, the book is referred to in its totality. Hence it is referred to by its author. In the footnote, the specific component of the book is referred to.)

Editor's foreword (preface or introduction) to an anthology

Bibliography
Hardy, John Edward, ed. "Foreword," *The Modern Talent.* New York: Holt, Rinehart & Winston, 1964.

Footnote
[13]John Edward Hardy, ed., "Foreword," *The Modern Talent* (New York: Holt, Rinehart & Winston, 1964), p. vi.

Classics: Plays

Bibliography
Hamlet.

Footnote
[14]*Hamlet* IV.vii.70–75.

(Note: Capital Roman numerals are acts; lower case Roman numerals scenes; Arabic numerals lines. Note that commas are not used after titles, and periods—not commas—separate main divisions.)

Classics: Poetry

Bibliography
Milton *Paradise Lost.*

Footnote
    ¹⁵Milton *Paradise Lost* V. 117-208.

(Note: Capital Roman numerals stand for books, Arabic numerals for lines. Note punctuation.)

The Bible

Bibliography
The Bible.

(Note: The Bible is never italicized.)

Footnote
    ¹⁶Psalms 12:3–6.

(Note: Parts of the Bible are never italicized; in this example, "12" is the chapter, and "3–6" are verses.)

ENCYCLOPEDIA ARTICLES

Signed article, general encyclopedia, alphabetically arranged

Bibliography
Brodie, Bernard. "Command of the Pacific." *Encyclopaedia Britannica,* 1960.

Footnote
    ¹⁷Bernard Brodie, "Command of the Pacific," *Encyclopaedia Britannica,* 1960.

(Note: No volume and page numbers are required when the reference work is alphabetically arranged. No place of publication and publisher are needed for any general encyclopedia.)

Unsigned article, general encyclopedia, alphabetically arranged

Bibliography

"Pacific Grove." *Encyclopaedia Britannica,* 1960.

Footnote

[18]"Pacific Grove," *Encyclopaedia Britannica,* 1960.

Signed article, specialized encyclopedia, alphabetically arranged

Bibliography

Acton, H. B. "The Absolute." *Encyclopedia of Philosophy.* New York: Macmillan, 1967.

Footnote

[19]H. B. Acton, "The Absolute," *Encyclopedia of Philosophy* (New York: Macmillan, 1967).

MAGAZINES, NEWSPAPERS

Signed article

Bibliography

Moskowitz, Ron. "Brown Helps Get Campus Beer OKd." San Francisco *Chronicle,* 30 May 1975, Sec. 1, p. 1, cols. 6-7; p. 20, cols. 6-7.

Footnote

[20]Ron Moskowitz, "Brown Helps Get Campus Beer OKd," San Francisco *Chronicle,* 30 May 1975, Sec. 1, p. 1, col. 6.

(Note: Bibliography cites entire article. Footnote gives only that portion actually used in research paper.)

Bibliography

Striecher, Lawrence H. "David Low and the Mass Press." *Journalism Quarterly,* 43, No. 2 (Summer 1966), 211-20.

Footnote

[21]Lawrence H. Striecher, "David Low and the Mass Press," *Journalism Quarterly,* 43, No. 2 (Summer 1966), 215.

(Note: Volume numbers are frequently applied to scholarly journals that appear monthly, quarterly, or annually. In the above citation, "43" is the volume number and "No. 2" is the issue number of that volume. Page designation—*p.* or *pp.*—is dropped when volume number is used.)

Unsigned article

Bibliography

"The Mystery of Sudden Infant Death." *Consumer Reports,*
    June 1975, pp. 363–65.

Footnote

[22]"The Mystery of Sudden Infant Death," *Consumer Reports,* June 1975, p. 363.

Editorial

Bibliography

Editorial. San Francisco *Chronicle,* 29 May 1975, Sec. 3, p. 36,
    cols. 1-2.

Footnote

[23]Editorial, San Francisco *Chronicle,* 29 May 1975, Sec. 3,
p. 36, cols. 1-2.

MISCELLANEOUS

Pamphlet with author

Bibliography

Fredrickson, Donald T. *How to Stop Smoking!* New York:
    American Heart Association, 1969.

Footnote

[24]Donald T. Fredrickson, *How to Stop Smoking!* (New
York: American Heart Association, 1969), p. 2.

Pamphlet without author

Bibliography

The Heart and Blood Vessels. New York: American Heart
    Association, 1973.

Footnote

[25]*The Heart and Blood Vessels* (New York: American Heart Association, 1973), pp. 13–15.

Interview

Bibliography

Interview with three convicted plagiarists. San Mateo County Jail. Redwood City, Ca., June 20, 1976.

Footnote

[26]Interview with three convicted plagiarists, San Mateo County Jail, Redwood City, Ca., June 20, 1976.

Speech

Bibliography

Platt, Bradley K. "Colombian Cuisine." Ames, November 21, 1976. (Speech delivered at Iowa State University Student Union.)

Footnote

[27]Bradley K. Platt, "Colombian Cuisine," Speech delivered at Iowa State University Student Union, Ames, November 21, 1976.

Sample Research Paper

MARY CASSATT: INDEPENDENT IMPRESSIONIST

Rebecca Tomin

English 61.5
Dr. Elsohn
March 15, 1976

MARY CASSATT: INDEPENDENT IMPRESSIONIST

In 1860, when Mary Cassatt was sixteen, well-
brought-up young ladies learned to do a bit of genteel
painting--possibly a china plate or two, possibly a
fan, possibly a pale water color sketch of a pretty
garden. The one thing they did <u>not</u> do was to become
professional artists. It would have ruined their repu-
tations. But Mary Cassatt was determined. In fact,
many years later, her chauffeur, Armand Delapert, said
of her, "she was strong-willed in character, voice
strong, dry, at the same time sympathetic."[1] So it
was that at age sixteen she faced her father and told
him that she planned to go to Europe to study art and
become a professional artist. Thus began the life of
one who would be called "an emancipated woman at a
time when emancipated women were rare."[2] Perhaps her
emancipation never stretched beyond her work, but in
her art she was clearly independent; she was her own
"woman."

[1]Frederick A. Sweet, "America's Greatest Woman
Painter," <u>Vogue</u>, 15 Feb. 1954, p. 103.

[2]Robin McKown, <u>The World of Mary Cassatt</u> (New York:
Thomas Y. Crowell, 1972), p. 89.

She convinced her father to let her study abroad. When she got there she studied independently; she rejected the Salon--and the conventional art of her time--in favor of the advanced ideas of the Impressionists, who, incidentally, preferred to be called the Independents. While she utilized those parts of Impressionist theory that worked for her, she rejected many of their tenets that did not. Finally that independence in taste led to the introduction of Impressionist art to important collections in the United States.

Failing at first to convince her father to send her abroad, Cassatt spent four years at the Pennsylvania Academy of Fine Arts in Philadelphia. Papa's reluctance to send her to Europe in 1860 was due in some part to a Civil War, just then under way. In addition, Mr. Cassatt "could not comprehend the idea of the daughter of a gentleman having any thought of making painting a career. . . . To him it was unthinkable for a young woman of means and social position to go out into the world as an artist."[3] As a result, Mary Cassatt spent the next four years studying art in Philadelphia. For her the curriculum was meager. However, she dili-

[3]Frederick A. Sweet, <u>Miss Mary Cassatt Impressionist from Pennsylvania</u> (Norman, Oklahoma: University of Oklahoma Press, 1966), p. 17.

gently studied what was offered: an antique class, a life class, a series of lectures in anatomy, and experiences in copying from examples in the Academy's permanent collection. There is on record a permit granted to "Miss Cassatt to copy a portion of picture <u>Deliverance of Leyden</u> by Wittkamp. . . .Copying even a portion of a Wittkamp must have been as tedious in its way as the constant drawing from dull, lifeless casts."[4] It was hardly a suitable course of training for the likes of Mary Cassatt. Finally, in 1866, Mr. Cassatt gave in and consented to let her go abroad. Thus her determination led to her emancipation--up to a point. She went to Paris, all right, but with her mother. In Paris she stayed with family friends and was surrounded by other "proper" influences. Indeed, before long her father, mother, and sister moved permanently to Paris.

Thus began Mary's real years of preparation--the years of independent study in Paris, Parma, Seville, Madrid, Antwerp, and Haarlem. They were years of very hard work. After a brief stay at the atelier of Charles Chaplin--"suave, academic, and over lush"[5]--she decided that it must be her lot to go it alone, to study independently. Rather than studying at the Ecole des

[4]Ibid.

[5]Ibid., p. 18.

Beaux-Arts in Paris, she copied paintings at the Louvre
and other museums, choosing carefully the styles she
wished to emulate--a far cry from copying the likes of
Wittkamp.

Actually, Mary's progress in art was quite slow:
"she deliberately chose the long and difficult way--the
way she considered the soundest. . . .She believed
that too much art-school instruction was dangerous lest
a teacher impose his own style on her."[6] This did
develop her own style, but it certainly delayed her
when it came to mastering the techniques of painting.
After a trip back to Philadelphia (to avoid the Franco-
Prussian war), Cassatt went to Italy, primarily to Parma
where she studied the paintings of Correggio--"'Going to
school to Correggio' as she called it."[7] Of Correggio's
great dome in the Cathedral of Parma it has been said
that "there emanated directly from Correggio's paint an
intoxicating effect that can almost make one forget the
supremely successful realism in his description of attitudes and heads. . . .This art depends upon a knowledge
of the essence of color."[8] No wonder, then, that Mary

[6]Ibid., p. 25.

[7]Lillian Freedgood, Great Artists of America (New
York: Thomas Y. Crowell, 1963), p. 151.

[8]Oscar Hagen, Art Epochs and Their Leaders (New York:
Charles Scribner's Sons, 1927), p. 46.

5

Cassatt was attracted to the art of the Impressionist group upon her eventual return to Paris in 1874.

But from Parma, she went first to Seville where she did what are considered her first important paintings. These were Offrant le Panal au Torero and Toreador, both painted in 1873. Another painting, Pendant le Carnival, had already been accepted by the Paris Salon in 1872, quite a distinction. While in Spain she saw the paintings by Rubens at the Prado in Madrid. She was so impressed that she determined to go to Antwerp to study the work of Frans Hals. At Haarlem she copied Hals' Meeting of the Officers of the Cluveniers-Doelen --not a stroke-for-stroke copy, but a free one which managed to capture the feeling that Hals had evoked. In later years she was very proud of this copy and used to show it to young art students, assuring them that such an exercise was essential for their development.[9] It is possible that some of the impetus for doing such a copy might well have come from seeing Rubens' copies of Titian paintings in the Prado--done freely in just such a way.

[9]Sweet, Miss Mary Cassatt Impressionist from Pennsylvania, p. 27.

Mary Cassatt was now 30 years old, her professional career launched by virtue of the acceptance of her paintings in 1872 and 1873 by the Salon. Within a few years, however, she would reject the system--the Salon and all it stood for--in favor of exhibiting independently with the Impressionists. The importance of this can not be over-emphasized, for in Paris the power of the Salon over the career of the artist was absolute. So absolute was it that those not accepted for the annual show could not sell their work. Dealers would not handle their canvases; collectors would not buy them. Good art, to the judges of 1872, meant art that was academic, classical, conventional, conservative.[10] Even though nine years before, in 1863, there had been a scandal that resulted in Napoleon III ordering a showing of rejected art--the "Salon des Refusés"--the power of the Salon still held.

But times were beginning to change. And the stage was set when in 1874 a group of painters, not academic, not classical, certainly not conventional, decided to form a new group, which they called <u>Societé Anonyme des Artistes, Peintres, Sculpteurs, Graveurs, etc.</u> Under this name they showed the work of Manet, Monet, Degas,

[10]McKown, p. 20.

Pissarro, Morrissot, and others whose theories were to overturn the world of art. Fresh from studying the colors of Correggio and Rubens, Mary was ready for the new ideas that seemed to carry the work of those masters at least one step beyond. Most important, it was among the Impressionists--the name they came to be called by--that she discovered the work of Degas.

At about the same time that she discovered the genius of Degas, he had discovered hers. That took place in the Salon of 1874, to which she had sent the painting Madame Cortier. Degas said to a friend, "Here is someone who feels as I do."[11] This feeling flowered into friendship three years later when in 1877 Degas "finally came to see her with a mutual friend, Tourny."[12] He asked her to join the group of Impressionists and exhibit with them. She agreed and was determined never again to send a picture to the Salon, especially after her experience in 1875 when a portrait of her sister was rejected because the judges thought it was too bright! She toned it down, and, lo and behold, the following year, it was accepted.

[11]Ibid., p. 23.

[12]Sweet, Miss Mary Cassatt, p. 32.

Even though Mary Cassatt is linked with the Impressionist school, she really never was a rank-and-file Impressionist. She was her own "woman"; that is, she painted plain and sometimes charmless people in classically noble poses and with the same care that earlier artists lavished on saints and goddesses.[13] Degas probably admired her work first and foremost because she was a good draftsman and as interested as he in the form and movement of the human body. This was in opposition to one of the basic theories of Impressionism. The Impressionists preferred to portray landscapes rather than people. They preferred modeling by color alone rather than by line. They preferred outdoor scenes to indoor ones.[14] Cassatt did, however, absorb and transmute those parts of Impressionist theory that suited her independent taste, just as she absorbed and transmuted the assymetrical composition of the Japanese prints that were being shown in Paris at the time. One of the paintings she sent to the Fourth Impressionist Exhibition April 10-May 11, 1879, was La Loge--a distinguished pic-

[13]E. J. Ballard, "An American in Paris: Mary Cassatt," American Artist, March 1973, p. 45.

[14]Maurice Serullaz, French Painting: The Impressionist Painters, trans. W. J. Strachan (New York: Universe Books, n.d.), p. 6.

ture of a beautiful young lady. While the color suggests
the work of Renoir, the modeling and the glow are her
own. At the height of her powers in the 1880s and 1890s,
she concentrated on

> pictures for which she would in time be-
> come famous--portrayals of women engaged
> in the many attitudes of the life she
> knew so well, attending the theater,
> serving tea, having a fitting at the dress-
> maker's or trying on a hat. She also be-
> gan the first of many canvases and pastel
> drawings on the theme of mother and child
> . . . she saw the loveliness of each
> commonplace attitude. . .and rendered
> [it] with truth and beauty.[15]

Among those pictures are At the Opera now in the Boston
Museum of Fine Arts; The Cup of Tea in the Metropolitan
Museum in New York; The Bath in the Art Institute of
Chicago; The Boating Party in the National Gallery in
Washington, D.C.; Mother and Child at the Wichita Art
Museum; and Young Women Picking Fruit at the Carnegie
Institute of Pittsburgh. Her works also hang in the Jeu
de Paume in Paris, as well as in art museums in other
European cities.

Not only is Mary Cassatt remembered for her works of
art, but also for the fact that she was largely responsible for introducing Impressionist art to the United States.
In 1900, on her first trip to the U. S. in thirty years,
appalled by the poverty of the art collections, she took

[15]Freedgood, p. 156.

it upon herself to remedy the situation. On returning to
Paris, she called upon her wealthy American friends to
buy European masterworks, especially the moderns, i.e.,
Impressionists, "for the enrichment of their native
land."[16] To this end, she offered her services as ex-
pert. Thus it was that in 1901 her dear friends mil-
lionaire sugar magnate Henry O. Havemeyer and his wife
Louisine, in Europe on an art buying trip, asked Mary to
accompany them so that they could use her judgment in
buying paintings in Italy and Spain. Mary had known Mrs.
Havemeyer from the time she was a seventeen-year-old
school girl in Paris and had helped her to buy her first
painting of note, La Repetition de Ballet by Degas.
This painting formed the basis for what was to become one
of the great art collections of the United States. Some
of the results of the trip of 1901 were the purchase of
paintings by Velasquez, El Greco (View of Toledo and
Assumption of the Virgin, among others),[16] Veronese,
Lippi, and Goya. But Mary could hardly let the Havemeyers go before she introduced them to the art dealers
Durand-Ruel and Ambroise Vollard who handled works of the
Impressionists. As a result, Henry and Louisine bought

[16]Freedgood, p. 159.

over the years thirty-five paintings by Courbet and a
large number of works by Monet, Manet, Cezanne, Renoir,
and others of the Impressionist group. The Havemeyer
collection was eventually bequeathed to the Metropolitan
Museum of Art in New York.[17]

The Havemeyers were not the only persons who learned
about the Impressionists from Mary Cassatt. In 1881 she
had bought a Pissarro and a Monet for her brother,
Alexander, now president of the Pennsylvania Railroad.
This she considered a good investment for her family. As
time went on, Alexander, who never really appreciated
art, bought, at her insistence, many other Impressionist
paintings. Many years later Mary wrote his son, Robert,
"that the paintings must be worth at least $200,000--
hundreds of times more than he paid for them."[18] In the
years after 1901, she assisted many collectors such as
Mrs. Potter Palmer and especially James Stillman, who was
president of the National City Bank of New York, in
assembling their collections of art. In all these cases,
it was principally Impressionist art that she recommended.
In recognition of her efforts, one American newspaper,
the New York Herald-Tribune, gave Mary Cassatt special

[17]Sweet, "America's Greatest Woman Painter," p. 103.
[18]Ballard, p. 47.

credit for "drawing the attention of her countrymen to the
merits of her French colleagues."[19]

As time went on, the honors began to arrive, along
with the compliments. In 1904 the Walter Lippincott Prize
of the Pennsylvania Academy of Fine Arts was awarded her
for her painting The Caress, which is now in the Smith-
sonian Institution National Collection of Fine Arts.
This award was the first of many which she declined. In
her reply to the director of the Academy she said that as
one of the founders of the Independents she must stick to
her principles which were "no jury, no medals, no
awards. . . ."[20] Toward the end of 1904 came the most
coveted honor. She was made a Chevalier de la Legion
d'Honneur. The only honor other than the ribbon of the
Legion that she felt able to accept was awarded her at the
close of her painting career in 1914 when the Pennsylvania Academy gave her the Gold Medal of Honor for
"eminent services to the Academy." Because the award was
to her as an artist rather than to any single painting,
she accepted it.

Toward the end of her life, her vision gone, unable

[19]McKown, p. 114.

[20]Sweet, Miss Mary Cassatt Impressionist from
Pennsylvania, p. 165.

to paint any longer, she was described as "acid tongued, contentious, a vinegary old maid."[21]   She, who had been in the front of the "avant garde," now disapproved of everything in art that came after the work of Cezanne. She criticized her friends, denounced Woodrow Wilson and Clemenceau for the Versailles Treaty, and was convinced that American students should not come to Europe to study but should remain in America and keep an American outlook. "Her own woman," independent to the last, she died in 1926 survived by her children--more than 225 prints and 940 paintings, pastels and watercolors--to seal her reputation as an artist of the first rank.

[21]Freedgood, p. 162.

Bibliography

Ballard, E. J. "An American in Paris: Mary Cassatt."
    American Artist, March 1973, pp. 40-47.

"Best U.S. Painter: Mother and Child." Time, 12 October
    1953, pp. 92-93.

Bizardel, Yvon. American Painters in Paris. New York:
    Macmillan, 1960.

Drexler, R. "Mary Cassatt in Washington: Exhibition at
    the National Gallery." Life, 30 October 1970, p. 10.

Freedgood, Lillian, Great Artists of America. New York:
    Thomas Y. Crowell, 1963.

Hagen, Oscar. Art Epochs and Their Leaders. New York:
    Charles Scribner's Sons, 1927.

McKown, Robin. The World of Mary Cassatt. New York:
    Thomas Y. Crowell, 1972.

Serullaz, Maurice. French Painting: The Impressionist
    Painters. Trans. W. J. Strachan. New York: Universe
    Books, n.d.

Sweet, F. A. "America's Greatest Woman Painter." Vogue,
    February 1954, pp. 102-103.

_____. Miss Mary Cassatt Impressionist from Pennsylvania.
    Norman, Oklahoma: University of Oklahoma Press, 1966.

Wilenski, R. H. Modern French Painters. New York: Har-
    court Brace Jovanovich, n.d.

Wilson, Ellen. American Painter in Paris: A Life of Mary
    Cassatt. New York: Farrar, Strauss & Giroux, 1971.

Appendix B

Glossary of Usage

This glossary discusses in brief a generous selection of the words and constructions that may confuse students who use this handbook. We have attempted to be useful and practical instead of comprehensive, since the scope of our little handbook is necessarily restricted to the most troublesome writing problems confronting college students.

It is important to note that only General English, a variety of Standard English, can be recommended as appropriate to most college writing. See the main entry on **Usage** for a more detailed outline of the characteristics of Standard and Nonstandard English. For convenience we will define the following terms here:

1. *Standard English:* the spoken and written language of educated men and women; comprising General English, Informal English, and Formal English.

2. *Nonstandard English:* the language of illiterate people, of certain dialect groups, and of some minorities.

3. *Informal English:* the language used by educated people in private conversations, personal letters, and writing intended to be close to popular speech; a variety of Standard English.

4. *General English:* the spoken and written language of the educated majority; essentially a literary language used in business letters, book reviews, student essays and examinations, professional fiction and nonfiction of all sorts, and an extensive variety of other writing. The vocabulary of General English consists largely of those words *not* marked by usage labels in dictionaries.

5. *Formal English:* essentially a written language, characterized by a precise, extensive vocabulary, with a high proportion of words derived from Latin and Greek; appropriate to technical, scientific, and academic writing; less occasionally appropriate to student writing (the Formal vocabulary and constructions often seem wooden, stilted, and pretentious, especially in the prose of beginning writers).

6. *Colloquial:* belonging to the constructions and idioms of conversation and informal writing; not appropriate to most college writing; definitely not appropriate to formal writing.

7. *Slang:* "the body of words and expressions frequently used by or intelligible to a rather large portion of the general American public, but not accepted as good, formal usage by the majority" (Stuart Berg Flexner, *Dictionary of American Slang*). Under most circumstances, slang is not acceptable in college writing.

In preparing this glossary of usage we have consulted the following reference works: *Webster's Third New International Dictionary, Webster's New World Dictionary of the American Language* (Second Edition), *The American*

Heritage Dictionary of the English Language, A Dictionary of Contemporary American Usage by Bergen Evans and Cornelia Evans, *Dictionary of American Slang* by Harold Wentworth and Stuart Berg Flexner, and *The Oxford English Dictionary.*

A, an. Use *a* before words beginning with a consonant or a sounded *h: a book, a lighter, a pair, a hotel.* Use *an* before words beginning with a vowel or vowel sound: *an ant, an hour, an orange.*

Accept, except. Do not confuse. *Accept* is always a verb meaning "to take or receive": "I accepted Donna's gift with pleasure." *Except* may be either a verb or a preposition. As a verb it means "to exclude": "The instructor excepted only a few students from the exam." As a preposition *except* means "leaving out": "Everyone was happy except Fred."

Ad. Colloquial shortening of *advertisement.* Prefer the full word.

Ain't. Nonstandard (often dialectal) contraction of *am not, are not, has not, have not.* Sometimes used for shock value in educated speech. Do not use in college writing.

Affect, effect. Do not confuse. Most commonly *affect* means "to influence": "Your grade will be affected by class participation." *Effect,* as a verb, means "to cause to happen; to bring about": "The medicine effected the desired result." *Effect* is also a noun meaning "result": "The effect of stress on the production of hormones is now being studied by medical researchers."

Alibi. Colloquial for *excuse.* Standard only in the legal sense of "the plea or fact that an accused person was elsewhere than at the alleged scene of the offense with which he is charged."

All right, alright. The correct spelling is *all right. Alright* is Nonstandard—and is almost always considered a misspelling.

Alot. Misspelling of *a lot. Alot* occurs with amazing frequency. Avoid!

Among, between. Among always indicates more than two: "There was real friendship among members of that English class." *Between* generally designates only two ("Between Jim and me there is enough money for bread and cheese") but may be used, according to the *Oxford English Dictionary,* "to express the relation of a thing to many surrounding things severally and individually," as in "a treaty between three powers."

Amount, number. Use *amount* to express quantity, bulk, or mass, *number* to refer to countable items: "a large amount of flour" but "a number of apples."

And etc. Redundant: *etc.* is an abbreviation of the Latin phrase *et cetera,* "and other [things]." *Et* MEANS "and."

Anyways. Dialectal (Nonstandard) for *anyway* or *in any case:* "I may not do well in French, but I try *anyway."*

As. Overused and imprecise when substituted for *because* or *since* to introduce a clause. Prefer "I didn't work in the garden because I was tired" to "I didn't work in the garden as I was tired."

As to. Wordy. Prefer *about:* "I don't know about that date, but I'll check my calendar."

Awful, awfully. Awful, in the sense of "very bad," is colloquial. "The food was awful" might be acceptable under some circumstances, but "The food was abominable" would generally be preferred. *Awfully,* meaning "extremely" or "very," as in "I was awfully excited," is also colloquial.

Bad, badly. Bad is an adjective, *badly* an adverb: use *bad* after a linking verb ("I feel bad tonight") and *badly* with action verbs ("Cohn behaved badly when he beat Pedro Romero"). *Badly* in the sense of "very much" is colloquial: "Jake needed Brett very much (not *badly*)."

Being as. Nonstandard for *since, because.* Do *not* write "Being as I was very hungry, I ordered a dozen oysters, a seafood salad, the assorted shell-fish platter, a bottle of Blue Nun, cheese cake, and a pot of coffee." Begin "Since (or *because*) I was very hungry. . . ."

Beside, besides. Beside means "by the side of": "I sat beside Martha St. John." *Besides* means "in addition to": "Besides me, there were Jonathan Wild, Martha St. John, and Gilmore Stern."

Between. See *Among, between.*

Broke. Colloquial in the sense of "without money."

Bunch. Colloquial in the sense of "group" or "gathering," as in "a bunch of people."

Bust, busted, bursted. Nonstandard forms of *burst;* present and past tenses and the past participle are all spelled *burst.*

Can, may. Can means "be able to"; *may* means "have permission to": "Lisa can sing well." "May I sing tonight?" *Can* in the sense of "have permission" is colloquial.

Can't hardly. Nonstandard (dialectal): a double negative. Use *can hardly.*

Complected. Colloquial or dialectal for *complexioned.* Prefer the latter.

Considerable. An adjective: "I spent a considerable amount of money last month." Do not use as an adverb, as in "I like her considerable."

Contact. Many people sensitive to language object to using *contact* as a verb. Prefer *arrange to meet, consult, talk with,* or even (if you must) *make contact with.*

Continual, continuous. Distinguish between these two words. *Continual* means "occurring repeatedly; going on in rapid succession": "Laura's continual interruptions annoyed Professor Thrumbottom." *Continuous* means "extending without interruption in either space or time": "We can measure but not really feel the continuous movement of the earth around the sun."

Contractions. Though slightly informal, contractions such as *won't, can't,* and *haven't* are usually acceptable in General English despite objections from purists and conservatives. Contractions are not appropriate, of course, in highly formal writing.

Could of. Nonstandard for *could have.*

Data. Plural of *datum,* which is almost never used. *Data* is often treated as a singular, however, as in "This data is misleading."

Definitely. Often objected to as imprecise and overused in the sense of "positively, certainly": "I'm certainly (not *definitely*) going to visit my hometown next summer."

Different than. Now considered colloquial. Prefer *different from,* as in "I am an individual, different from every other person who has ever lived."

Due to. Do not use in the sense of *because of* or *owing to;* there is strong and not entirely unreasonable prejudice against such use: "Because of (not *due to*) the long day in the sun, my cat Mephisto seemed quite contented with life." There is no objection to the use of *due* as an adjective: "My check is due soon."

Effect. See *Affect, effect.*

Either, neither. Designates one of two (not one of more than two): "Either of these [two] dictionaries is satisfactory" but "Not one of these [three] books is appropriate."

Emigrate, immigrate. Emigrate means "to leave one country or region to settle in another." *Immigrate* means "to come into a new country in order to settle there."

Enthuse. A colloquial substitute for "be enthusiastic." Avoid such usages as "My friends are enthused about my role in *American Graffiti*."

Etc. Abbreviation of the Latin phrase *et cetera,* "and other [things]." Do not use *etc.* carelessly or loosely; instead, make a real effort to develop your ideas with effective details. See *And etc.*

Expect. Colloquial in the sense of "suppose" or "suspect."

Farther, further. Generally, *farther* is used to express distance and *further* to mean "in addition; more." "The ball went farther than I thought it would" but "Further discussion of your grade is pointless."

Faze. A colloquial verb meaning "to disturb, disconcert." Do not confuse *faze* with the noun *phase.*

Fewer, less. *Fewer* is used with numbers, *less* with degree, value, or amount. "Fewer than thirty people attended the game." "Our dinner at Spenger's cost less than we thought it would." Note: the sign at the supermarket check-out counter should read: "EXPRESS LANE— FEWER (not *less*) THAN EIGHT ITEMS." Combat imprecise language.

Fix. Most commonly means "to make firm, stable, or secure." Dialectal or colloquial in the sense of "prepare, intend," as in "I'm fixing to do my homework."

Funny. Colloquial for *strange, odd, queer.*

Guy. Colloquial for *boy* or *man.* Used carelessly, imprecisely, and far too frequently. Do not use this word in college writing.

Hang. An object is *hung;* a person is *hanged* (executed). The principal parts are *hang, hung, hung* (object) and *hang, hanged, hanged* (person).

Hisself. Nonstandard for *himself.*

Imply, infer. To imply is "to suggest": "The instructor implied that his students didn't write well." *To infer* is "to draw a conclusion": "The students inferred that their instructor was dissatisfied with their writing."

In, into. In means "located within": "I was standing in the room." *Into* denotes "motion to a point within": "Sam walked into the room."

Infer. See *Imply, infer.*

Irregardless. Nonstandard for *regardless.*

Its, it's. Its is the possessive pronoun. *It's* is the contraction of *it is.* Do not confuse these words: to do so is inexcusable.

Just. Colloquial when used in the sense of *simply* or *completely,* as in "I was just [simply] teasing."

Kind of, sort of. Colloquial for *somewhat, rather:* "The children were kind of [rather] excited about their trip to Bear Valley."

Lay, lie. In the most common uses, *lay* is a transitive verb meaning "set, place." *Lie* is an intransitive verb meaning "recline." (Transitive verbs take direct objects; intransitive verbs do not.)

The principal parts of *lay* are *lay* (present tense), as in "Lay the book on the desk"; *laid* (past tense), as in "Margo laid the book on the desk"; *laid* (past participle), as in "The concrete was laid yesterday." The principal parts of *lie* are *lie* (present tense), as in "Lie down"; *lay* (past tense), as in "I lay down for an hour"; *lain* (past participle), as in "I have lain here for an hour." *Lay* and *lie* are not particularly difficult words for those who take the time to learn the differences between them and who care enough about language to want to use it precisely and correctly. We urge you to learn—and to care.

Less. See *Fewer, less.*

Lie. See *Lay, lie.*

Like, as, as if. In General English observe the following distinctions: *Like* (preposition): "She dresses like a mature, sophisticated woman." *As* (conjunction): "Do as (not *like*) I say." *As if* (conjunction): "This book looks as if (not *like*) it might make difficult reading."

In short, do not use *like* as a conjunction: it is colloquial; it wears the taint of commercial jargon; and there is strong prejudice against it, especially in slightly more formal shades of General English.

Lose, loose. Different in meaning and pronunciation. *Lose* means "to fail to keep." *Loose* as a verb means "to unbind, set free"; as an adjective, "free, unbound."

Lots, lots of. Colloquial for *many, much, a great deal of:* "Mr. Warburton makes a great deal of (not *lots of*) money."

Mad. Colloquial for *enraged, angry, furious,* although recorded in these senses as early as 1300 (*Oxford English Dictionary*). In Formal English *mad* means "insane."

May. See *Can, may.*

May of. Nonstandard for *may have.*

Mean. Colloquial for *bad-tempered, disagreeable, malicious.*

Might of. Nonstandard for *might have.*

Mighty. Colloquial in the sense of *very,* as in "I'm mighty pleased to meet you."

Most. In the sense of *nearly,* a colloquial form of *almost.* General English: "We visit Yosemite almost (not *most*) every summer."

Must of. Nonstandard for *must have.*

Neither. See *Either, neither.*

No place. Informal for *nowhere.*

Number, amount. See *Amount, number.*

Of. Nonstandard for *have* in such constructions as *could have, might have.*

Off of. Formerly in standard use but now dialectal. "I fell off (not *off of*) the balcony."

OK, O.K., okay. Colloquial for *satisfactory, all right, correct.*

Ought to of. Nonstandard for *ought to have.*

Out loud. Frequently considered colloquial. Prefer *aloud* in more formal writing.

Per. Correctly used in *per pound, per foot,* etc. *As per* is redundant—and tainted by commercial use. Avoid "as per instructions" and similar phrases.

Phone. Considered colloquial. Use *telephone* in more formal writing.

Photo. Colloquial form of *photograph.* Use the full word in more formal writing.

Plenty. Informal when used as an adverb.
Informal: "The redwoods are plenty tall."
General: "The redwoods are certainly tall."

Prefer. Usually followed by *to:* "I prefer this to that." Do not follow by *than,* as in "I prefer steak than seafood."

Pretty. Generally accepted for *moderately, fairly,* or *somewhat,* but weakened by overuse. Vary it by judiciously chosen synonyms.

Principal, principle. Do not confuse. *Principal* as an adjective means "chief, main, first in rank or authority"; as a noun, "governing or presiding officer." *Principle,* a noun, means "ultimate source; fundamental truth or law."

Prof. Slang when used as common noun in place of *professor,* as in "The prof mutters in a low, monotonous voice." The best practice is to write the word in full on all occasions: "Professor Jones is a brilliant lecturer."

Quiet, quite. Quiet is an adjective meaning "motionless, hushed." *Quite* is an adverb meaning "completely, entirely." Do not confuse.

Real. Colloquial as an intensive adverb meaning *really* or *very*, as in "The steak was real good."

Reason is because. General English requires *reason is that.*
Colloquial: "The reason you don't sleep well is because you don't get enough exercise."
General English: "The reason you don't sleep well is that you don't get enough exercise."

Reckon. Dialectal or colloquial for *believe, suppose, think,* as in "I reckon I'll do it if I want."

Right. As an intensive adverb meaning *very,* colloquial or dialectal (Southern U.S.): "He's a right smart boy." Prefer *very* in General English.

Raise, rise. *Raise* is a transitive verb; its principal parts are *raise, raised, raised:* "I have raised frangipanis for many years." *Rise* is an intransitive verb; its principal parts are *rise, rose, risen:* "I rise early on school mornings." "The sun rose at 6:13 A.M." "I had risen at 5:00 A.M. in order to write a lecture for my eight o'clock class."

Set, sit. Often confused. The principle parts of *set,* meaning "to place," are
set (present tense), as in "I now set the cup on the table";
set (past tense), as in "I set the cup on the table";
set (past participle), as in "I had set the cup on the table."
Set is perfectly clear, straightforward, and regular, but it is often confused with *sit. Sit* is usually an intransitive verb; its principal parts are
sit (present tense), as in "I now sit down";
sat (past tense), as in "I sat down";
sat (past participle), as in "I have sat [not *set*] down."
As noted, mistakes generally occur in the use of *set* for *sit.* Do not write "I am setting down," "Set down, friend," or "I set down to do my homework." All such usages are incorrect.

Should of. Nonstandard for *should have.*

Show up. Colloquial when used to mean "be superior to," as in "Our team showed up the Cougars."

So. Overused as a coordinating conjunction, as in "It was a sunny day, so we went to the beach." Try to achieve variety by substituting conjunctive adverbs for *so*-constructions: "Writing is hard work; consequently, I seldom write for more than four hours at a time." You can also make other changes in sentence structure: "It was such a sunny day that we went to the beach."

Some. Informal when used for *a little* or *somewhat,* as in "I rested some yesterday." Slang when used as an intensive. "He is some (meaning *superior*) student."

Sort of. See *Kind of, sort of.*

Such. Colloquial for *to a great degree,* as in "He is such a good teacher." This and similar constructions are careless and vague.

Swell. Slang for *very good, excellent,* as in "We ate at a swell French restaurant."

Terrible. Colloquial for *very bad.*

That there. Nonstandard for *that:* "That (not *that there*) song brings back sad memories."

Their, there, they're. Do not make an exhibit of your ignorance or carelessness by confusing these words. *Their* is a possessive pronoun, *there* an adverb, and *they're* the contraction for *they are.*

This here. Nonstandard for *this.*

Thusly. Pretentious. Prefer the simple form *thus.*

To, too, two. Do not confuse the preposition *to* ("to the cabin") with the adverb *too* ("too much to eat") or the numeral *two* ("two steaks"). Do not use *too* in the sense of *very,* as in "I am not too fond of him."

Unique. Means "one of its kind." Hence logically something cannot be "very unique" or "more unique." Although the informal senses of the word ("remarkable, uncommon") are clear enough, it is best to avoid them in General to Formal English.

Used to could. Nonstandard for *used to be able* (*could* does not have an infinitive form).

Wait on. Colloquial or dialectal when used to mean "wait for."

Ways. Informal for *distance*, as in "We have come quite a ways."

Where. Informal in such a sentence as "I read where almost no jobs are available for teachers." The accepted construction uses *that:* "I read that almost no jobs are available for teachers."

Where . . . at. Informal and redundant, as in "Do you know where Jon's at?" Prefer "Do you know where Jon is?"

Where . . . to. Informal and redundant, as in "Where are you going to?" Omit the *to.*

Which, who. Do not use *which* to refer to people: "Lisa is a girl who (not *which*) can sing and dance like a professional."

While. Overused as a conjunction when *and* or *but* would serve better. *While* most precisely designates time: "I wrote while my father read."

Would of. Nonstandard for *would have.*

You all. Dialectal for *you* (Southern U.S.).

Index